HILLSIDE PUBLIC LIBRARY

3 1992 00229 8702

W9-BBN-572

MAR 1 1 2020

HILLSIDE PUBLIC LIBRARY
405 N. HILLSIDE AVENUE
HILLSIDE, IL 60162
708-449-7510

LGBT Discrimination

Heidi C. Feldman

ReferencePoint
Press®

San Diego, CA

Oceanside Public Library

About the Author

Heidi C. Feldman is an author, editor, and educator. Her book about Afro-Peruvian music won the Woody Guthrie Book Prize from the International Association of Popular Music (US) and was published in Spanish translation in Peru. For seven years she was a volume editor for *Bloomsbury Encyclopedia of Popular Music of the World*. She has taught at San Diego State University, University of California–San Diego, Soka University of America, and Tulane University. She lives in San Diego with her family.

© 2019 ReferencePoint Press, Inc.
Printed in the United States

For more information, contact:
ReferencePoint Press, Inc.
PO Box 27779
San Diego, CA 92198
www.ReferencePointPress.com

ALL RIGHTS RESERVED.
No part of this work covered by the copyright hereon may be reproduced or used in any form or by any means—graphic, electronic, or mechanical, including photocopying, recording, taping, web distribution, or information storage retrieval systems—without the written permission of the publisher.

Picture Credits:

Cover: Elenabsl/Shutterstock.com

 5: Rawpixel.com/Shutterstock.com
10: lev radin/Shutterstock.com
14: Evan El-Amin/Shutterstock.com
16: Rawpixel.com/Shutterstock.com
24: Chris Tilley/Reuters/Newscom
28: Rick Wilking/Reuters/Newscom
31: Associated Press

35: Darren Baker/Shutterstock.com
39: Nancy Stone/TNS/Newscom
42: Charlie Neuman/ZUMA Press/Newscom
44: Maury Aaseng
48: Monkey Business Images/Shutterstock.com
55: David Poller/ZUMA Press/Newscom
58: Steve Nesius/Reuters/Newscom
60: Photographee.eu/Shutterstock.com
65: Ian Francis/Shutterstock.com

LIBRARY OF CONGRESS CATALOGING-IN-PUBLICATION DATA

Names: Feldman, Heidi Carolyn, 1965– author.
Title: LGBT Discrimination/by Heidi C. Feldman.
Description: San Diego, CA: ReferencePoint Press, Inc., [2019] | Series:
  Discrimination in Society | Includes bibliographical references and index.
  Identifiers: LCCN 2018017505 (print) | LCCN 2018018169 (ebook) | ISBN
  9781682823842 (eBook) | ISBN 9781682823835 (hardback)
Subjects: LCSH: Homophobia—United States—Juvenile literature. | Gay
  rights—United States—Juvenile literature. | Sexual minorities—Civil
  rights—United States—Juvenile literature. | Discrimination—United
  States—Juvenile literature.
Classification: LCC HQ76.45.U5 (ebook) | LCC HQ76.45.U5 F45 2019 (print) |
  DDC 306.76/60973—dc23
LC record available at https://lccn.loc.gov/2018017505

CONTENTS

LGBT in America: Both Personal and Public

In 2013 *Time* magazine featured an intimate close-up cover image of a same-sex couple kissing. The headline read: "Gay Marriage Already Won: The Supreme Court Hasn't Made Up Its Mind—but America Has." An article in *Harvard Business Review* that same year posed the question: "What Made Same-Sex Marriage Go Viral?"

This mainstream media coverage, two years before the landmark 2015 Supreme Court ruling that legalized gay marriage throughout the United States, is a reminder that being lesbian, gay, bisexual, or transgender (LGBT) in America is both a personal and a public issue. A person's sexual orientation and gender identity are private and personal matters. At the same time, especially since marriage equality, more people are making their LGBT status publicly known in their workplaces, schools, and neighborhoods. As a result, laws and policies about LGBT discrimination are an increasingly prominent and public issue.

How Many People Are LGBT in America?

Despite the growing public prominence of LGBT people, an accurate count of the LGBT population is lacking. Gary J. Gates of the Williams Institute, a University of California–Los Angeles School of Law think tank dedicated to LGBT issues, affirms that knowing how many people are LGBT in America would make them visible as an interest group to lawmakers and policy makers. For example, accurate statistics would help researchers determine to what extent LGBT people face barriers in accessing health care, whether they are assaulted at a higher rate than the general population, or whether elected officials adequately represent their concerns.

However, several challenges make it difficult to know exactly how many people are LGBT in America. First, over past decades, the wording of survey questions that seek to identify sexual orientation and gender identity has changed. This makes it problematic to arrive at a consensus regarding who counts as LGBT and to compare survey responses. Further, because of social stigma, it is very common for people to lie about their sexual orientation and gender identity on surveys and polls.

A gay couple dances at their wedding reception. In 2015 the US Supreme Court ruled that the Constitution guarantees a right to same-sex marriage.

While a completely accurate count may not be possible, available research suggests that the adult LGBT population in America is somewhere between 1.7 percent and 7.5 percent. In a 2017 Gallup poll, 4.1 percent of the US population identified as LGBT (around 10 million people, up from 3.5 percent in 2012). The Williams Institute estimates that 0.6 percent of US adults identify as transgender. Studies also show that a growing number of millennials identify and are coming out (making their identity known) publicly as LGBT. Also, more and more Americans—especially youth—identify as gender fluid, meaning that they do not always feel cisgender (people whose gender identity matches the sex assigned on their birth certificates).

LGBT and Other Names

A related difficulty in quantifying the LGBT population is the large number of names and acronyms that exist to describe them. The acronym *LGBT* emerged in the 1990s to emphasize the shared experiences of groups that identify with particular sexual orientations and gender identities. *LGBT* stands for "lesbian" (females attracted to females), "gay" (males and females attracted to members of the same sex), "bisexual" (males and females attracted to both sexes), and "transgender" (individuals who identify with a gender that does not match the sex assigned on their birth certificates).

LGBT is a dignified alternative to derogatory labels. Historically, the term *homosexual* was linked with efforts to criminalize people and to describe them as deviant, immoral, or mentally ill. In the 1940s and 1950s, the term *gay* emerged as a slang term to avoid the negative connotations of *homosexual*. The term *gay* was theoretically unisex but often used to apply to males. During the women's liberation movement of the 1960s and 1970s, many gay women identified separately as lesbians. Around 1965 the term *transgender* first appeared. In 1980 the American Psychiatric Association classified transgender identity as a mental disorder. The transgender rights movement emerged in the 1980s, and in the 1990s the acronym *GLBT* (later spelled LGBT) joined bisexual and transgender people with gays and lesbians.

In recent years alternate acronyms have been proposed, such as LGBTQ (the Q may stand for either "queer" or "questioning"). Some people prefer to identify with specific terms, even reclaiming terms previously used as insults, such as *queer*. Gerard Koskovich, curator at the San Francisco GLBT History Museum, notes the broader meaning of the public debate about names: "It's not just a debate about an acronym or a set of terminology. That's the proxy for a discussion about . . . people's ability to live in the world and feel that their experience and desire and sense of self is being honored."[1]

It is hurtful to many LGBT people when others, sometimes unknowingly, use incorrect or derogatory terms. Transgender people may experience painful identity denial when people do not use preferred pronouns. The antidefamation organization GLAAD publishes a media guide that includes a glossary of appropriate terms. The guide also lists terms to avoid, such as *homosexual* and *sexual preference*, and derogatory language such as *fag* or *dyke*.

> "It's not just a debate about an acronym or a set of terminology. That's the proxy for a discussion about . . . people's ability to live in the world and feel that their experience and desire and sense of self is being honored."[1]
>
> —Gerard Koskovich, curator at the San Francisco GLBT History Museum

The Consequences of Coming Out

Awareness of ongoing discrimination still causes many LGBT people to remain in the closet (keeping their LGBT status secret). Historically, the consequences of coming out as LGBT have in many cases been severe. Known LGBT people have been jailed, fired from jobs, and forced to undergo conversion therapy (a harmful practice that aims to "cure" LGBT people through usually inhumane means). They have been socially shunned, rejected by family, and classified as criminals and deviants.

A Center for American Progress report published in 2017 documented that more than one in four national LGBT respondents experienced discrimination in 2016 on the basis of their sexual orientation or gender identity. The consequences of coming out as LGBT included a greater risk of discrimination at work, at home, at school, in health care, and in public life. LGBT people of color and disabled LGBT people faced even higher rates of discrimination.

The Center for American Progress report also found that many LGBT people alter their public lives in order to avoid discrimination. For example, LGBT people use vague language when talking with coworkers and even family members about relationships. They hide affiliations and avoid discussion of LGBT topics in social situations. They move away from family and cut important people out of their lives. They make specific decisions about where to live, go to school, work, and shop. They avoid public transportation and doctors' offices. Clearly, LGBT discrimination in America is a public problem.

CHAPTER 1

Is LGBT Discrimination Against the Law?

Is it against the law in the United States to discriminate against LGBT people on the basis of their sexual orientation or gender identity? The answer is, it depends.

LGBT discrimination often falls into a legal gray area. This is because no federal laws clearly prohibit discrimination based on sexual orientation and gender identity, and state laws vary across the country. Sometimes, federal and state lawmakers disagree about LGBT rights, sending mixed messages to the public. Government leaders, legislators, and courts are still debating whether existing antidiscrimination and civil rights laws apply to LGBT people. For good reason, it often remains unclear to the average American whether discrimination against LGBT people is against the law.

The Battle for Marriage Equality

In the first part of the twenty-first century, the LGBT movement's main goal has been to attain federal rights. Central to this effort were the ups and downs in the long battle over same-sex marriage. In 1996 the federal Defense of Marriage Act defined marriage as a union between a man and a woman. Then in 2003 the Supreme Court struck down laws that made gay and lesbian sexual relations between consenting adults a crime. A few US states legalized gay marriage in the early 2000s. However, same-sex marriages performed in these states were not considered legal in other states, and several states explicitly banned gay marriage. Many LGBT people got married in one state but were unable to qualify for the legal benefits of marriage if they lived and worked in another state.

Two landmark Supreme Court cases finally legalized same-sex marriage all across America. First, in 2013 the Supreme Court ruling in *United States v. Windsor* brought marriage equality to thirteen US states and Washington, DC. In these states, while same-sex couples could marry legally, they were still denied tax breaks and other federal legal benefits enjoyed by opposite-sex married couples because the federal Defense of Marriage Act defined marriage as male-female unions. The plaintiff in *United States v. Windsor*, Edith Windsor (who was eighty-three years old when her case was decided in 2013), had lived with her partner, Thea Spyer, for forty years and nursed her through paralysis and

Edie Windsor (center) was a grand marshal in the Gay Pride Parade in New York City in 2013. Windsor sued the US government when it required her to pay estate taxes on her inheritance from her deceased wife.

multiple sclerosis. Spyer first proposed marriage to Windsor in 1967, but they did not marry until 2007, after Spyer suffered a heart attack and learned she had only a year to live. Same-sex marriage was legal at that time in Canada but not in their home state of New York. So they went to Canada to get married.

After Spyer died, Windsor discovered that she would have to pay over $300,000 in estate taxes on her inheritance from her wife. Heterosexual married couples were exempt from paying this tax after the death of a spouse. Because Windsor's same-sex marriage was not recognized in the United States, she was denied the marriage exemption. Windsor believed this was a violation of her rights. She sued the US government, and her case went all the way to the Supreme Court.

The *United States v. Windsor* Supreme Court ruling struck down part of the Defense of Marrlage Act as unconstitutional, and it provided Windsor and many other same-sex spouses with the same federal benefits and protections granted to all heterosexual married partners. The National LGBTQ Task Force wrote about the *Windsor* case:

> The significance of the *Windsor* decision cannot be overstated. For same-sex couples residing in a state that recognizes their marriage, the full spectrum of federal benefits will now be available to them. . . . And, perhaps most importantly, LGB individuals will no longer be robbed of the personhood and dignity that comes with a national government's refusal to recognize their relationships.[2]

Attorney and political strategist Richard Socarides later commented on the significance of this case in the fight for nationwide marriage equality: "After it was decided in her [Windsor's] favor . . . it set the Court on an unstoppable path toward its landmark ruling two years later, declaring a nationwide right to same-sex marriage equality."[3]

The Right to Marriage

Shortly after the *Windsor* decision in 2013, John Arthur and Jim Obergefell, who had lived together in Ohio as a gay couple for over twenty years, traveled to Maryland to wed. Same-sex marriage was legal in Maryland but not in Ohio. Arthur was dying of amyotrophic lateral sclerosis and wanted his life partner, Obergefell, to receive the legal benefits granted to married survivors after the death of a spouse. "Saying 'I thee wed' was the most beautiful moment of my life,"[4] recalls Obergefell, describing his wedding, which took place in the Maryland airport landing area.

Days later, Arthur and Obergefell learned that their marriage would not be legally recognized in Ohio. When he died, Arthur would still be considered single. Obergefell fought for his right to be recognized as Arthur's husband on the death certificate. Like Windsor's before him, his case went all the way to the Supreme Court, where he was the lead plaintiff in a joint case filed on behalf of same-sex couples from four US states. Ultimately, they prevailed in *Obergefell v. Hodges* (2015) with a path-changing Supreme Court ruling that was described by Fred Sainz of the Human Rights Campaign as "the largest conferral of rights on LGBT people in the history of our country."[5] *Obergefell v. Hodges* legalized same-sex marriage as a constitutional right under the equal protection and due process clauses of the Fourteenth Amendment in all fifty US states. Supreme Court justice Anthony Kennedy wrote in the majority opinion that excluding LGBT people from marriage rights "has the effect of teaching that gays and lesbians are unequal in important respects. It demeans gays and lesbians for the State to lock them out of a central institution of the Nation's society."[6]

Same-Sex Marriages in the United States

Same-sex couples quickly exercised their right to marry after the *Obergefell* ruling, some even participating in mass public wedding ceremonies. When Windsor's case went to the Supreme

Court in 2013, only 21 percent of all same-sex couples (about 230,000 couples) were married, according to the Williams Institute. After the *Obergefell* ruling for marriage equality in June 2015, 38 percent of same-sex couples (about 390,000) were married. By 2017 the Williams Institute found that over 1.1 million Americans were married to a same-sex partner.

These same-sex couples married for the same reasons as their non-LGBT counterparts. Over 80 percent of both LGBT and non-LGBT couples surveyed by the Pew Research Center say that love was a very important reason to get married, and over 70 percent cited companionship. Before marriage equality, LGBT couples were denied the right to publicly celebrate their love and commitment in a legally binding wedding. Windsor notes, "Marriage is a magic word. And it is magic throughout the world. It has to do with our dignity as human beings, to be who we are openly."[7]

> "Marriage is a magic word. And it is magic throughout the world. It has to do with our dignity as human beings, to be who we are openly."[7]
>
> —Edith Windsor, plaintiff in same-sex marriage lawsuit

Denying LGBT couples the right to marriage also restricted many other rights. With marriage comes access to health insurance through a spouse's employer, tax advantages, parenting rights, inheritance rights, exemption from property tax after the death of a spouse, and hundreds of other legal rights and benefits. Indeed, according to the Pew Research Center survey, twice as many LGBT couples as non-LGBT couples identified legal rights and benefits as a very important reason to get married.

Marriage equality was the most visible LGBT discrimination issue of its time in the late twentieth to early twenty-first centuries. As more Americans were exposed to same-sex marriages, public approval for marriage equality increased. By 2017 the Pew Research Center found that almost two-thirds of Americans supported allowing gay and lesbian couples to marry. This represents a huge increase since 2007, when 37 percent of Americans supported gay marriage. Marriage equality, however, was only the first step in the ongoing effort to secure lasting and comprehensive equal rights for LGBT people in America.

Federal Actions on LGBT Rights

Since the major focus of the LGBT rights movement in the United States in the 2000s has been federal rights, the president, Congress, and legal institutions play a vital role. President Barack Obama was the first US president to actively support LGBT rights. Obama made history when he used the word *gay* (in reference to sexual orientation) in his second inaugural address in 2013.

During Obama's administration, many new LGBT rights protections were implemented. The Obama administration appointed over 250 known LGBT officials to full-time and advisory positions in the executive branch—more than all of the previous presidential administrations combined. Obama also implemented landmark

President Barack Obama was the first US president to actively support LGBT rights. He made history when he used the word gay (in reference to sexual orientation) in his second inaugural address in 2013.

President Barack Obama's Historic 2015 State of the Union Address

President Barack Obama's 2015 State of the Union address was historic because of its reference to ending persecution of LGBT people. It was also the first time a president used the word *transgender* in such an address. Calling attention to the legal and policy reforms implemented by the Obama administration on behalf of LGBT people, these public acknowledgments made LGBT people feel visible and included as priorities in national politics. In this excerpt from his 2015 State of the Union address, Obama said to Americans:

> And there's one last pillar of our leadership, and that's the example of our values. As Americans, we respect human dignity, even when we're threatened, which is why I have prohibited torture, and worked to make sure our use of new technology like drones is properly constrained. It's why we speak out against the deplorable anti-Semitism that has resurfaced in certain parts of the world. It's why we continue to reject offensive stereotypes of Muslims, the vast majority of whom share our commitment to peace. That's why we defend free speech, and advocate for political prisoners, and condemn the persecution of women, or religious minorities, or people who are lesbian, gay, bisexual or transgender. We do these things not only because they are the right thing to do, but because ultimately they will make us safer.

Quoted in White House, Office of the Press Secretary, "Remarks by the President in State of the Union Address, January 20, 2015," press release, January 20, 2015. https://obamawhitehouse.archives.gov.

hiring and employment protections for LGBT federal contractors and the military and issued public school guidelines that allowed transgender students to use the bathrooms and locker rooms of their choice. When Edith Windsor died in 2017, Obama credited LGBT rights activists with influencing the federal government to support gay marriage. He observed, "Because people like Edie stood up, my administration stopped defending the so-called Defense of Marriage Act in the courts."[8]

Since 2017 the Donald Trump administration has sought to overturn many of the Obama-era LGBT protections. Some of these reversals have been challenged in court, raising important legal questions. This process illustrates the uncertain status of many federal LGBT rights.

Legal Questions

At the heart of federal debates about LGBT discrimination is Title VII of the federal 1964 Civil Rights Act, which prohibits discrimination based on race, color, religion, sex, and national origin. Sexual orientation and gender identity are not explicitly included in the list of categories protected under Title VII. Therefore, in court cases about whether LGBT people are protected from discrimination by the Civil Rights Act, the answer depends on differing legal interpretations of the word *sex*.

Sexual orientation is not explicitly referenced in the 1964 Civil Rights Act, which prohibits discrimination based on race, color, religion, and sex. This has created differing legal interpretations of the word *sex* in relation to LGBT discrimination cases.

Some lower court judges have interpreted the word *sex* in the Civil Rights Act as including sexual orientation and gender identity. Others interpret *sex discrimination* as limited to unequal treatment of women versus men. Two federal government agencies that advise the courts—the US Equal Employment Opportunity Commission (EEOC) and the US Department of Justice (DOJ)—have taken opposing sides on this question. The EEOC supports the inclusion of gender identity and sexual orientation as protected classes. The DOJ agreed with this position in 2014 under Obama. Then, under Trump, Attorney General Jeff Sessions publicly reversed the DOJ's position in 2017 to argue that *sex* means only male or female.

The Supreme Court has yet to rule on the question of whether LGBT people are protected from discrimination under the Civil Rights Act. While federal agencies, presidential administrations, and courts debate national policies and laws, LGBT discrimination continues unchecked in many US states.

The Battle for State Control

With no federal laws explicitly protecting all LGBT people from discrimination, many state governments actively seek to control LGBT rights within their borders. Immediately after gay marriage was legalized, a flood of LGBT rights bills followed at the state level. The American Civil Liberties Union (ACLU) reports that from 2013 to 2017 a total of 348 LGBT rights bills were introduced, and 23 became law. In 2018 only eight US states had not introduced any legislation limiting LGBT rights. In its 2017 report, the National Coalition of Anti-Violence Programs noted, "Recent efforts to pass sweeping anti-LGBTQ bills and rollbacks of protections leave LGBTQ communities vulnerable to identity-based discrimination and send the message that discriminating against LGBTQ people based on their identity and self-expression is both acceptable and legal."[9]

Among these state anti-LGBT bills, many religious liberty bills advocate that people who oppose homosexuality for religious

The First State to Legalize Same-Sex Marriage

Massachusetts became the first US state to legalize same-sex marriage in 2003. Seven same-sex couples had sued for the right to marry. In November 2003 the Massachusetts Supreme Judicial Court ruled that marriage equality is a constitutional right. The court gave state legislators 180 days to change state marriage licenses and rules accordingly.

The groundbreaking Massachusetts court decision was greeted with resistance that delayed its implementation. Both state governor Mitt Romney and US president George W. Bush advocated for constitutional amendments to limit the definition of marriage to male-female unions. Finally, on May 17, 2004, Marcia Kadish and Tanya McCloskey became the first same-sex partners legally married in the United States. Their wedding ceremony was held at Cambridge City Hall in Massachusetts. By the end of the day, seventy-seven other same-sex couples were married, and hundreds of applications had been submitted for marriage licenses.

In 2015 Massachusetts Supreme Judicial Court justice Margaret Marshall was asked whether she was surprised that same-sex marriage became legal throughout the United States only a little over a decade after her state court ruling. She explained that the first cases in the long fight for marriage equality had been filed in court fifty years earlier: "If you were a same-sex couple wanting to marry, wanting to declare your love, in the 1950s, it's been a long time coming. To my grandchildren who are now in their early 20s, they can't understand why there's any issue about it."

Quoted in Martha Bebinger, "Where It Began: Mass. Reacts to Supreme Court's Landmark Gay Marriage Ruling," WBUR News, June 26, 2015. www.wbur.org.

reasons should be allowed to discriminate against LGBT people without legal penalty. Marriage refusal bills seek to protect government employees and religious individuals who refuse to perform same-sex marriages. Bathroom bills intend to limit the ability of transgender people to use bathrooms corresponding with their gender identity (rather than the sex assigned on their birth certificates). While only a small number of these bills have become law, the dramatic increase of proposed bills since marriage equality reveals the aggressive battle for state control over LGBT rights.

The existence and level of LGBT legal protections varies from state to state (and even in different areas within states). New York, California, Maryland, and Oregon tend to be more LGBT-friendly, with a higher level of laws promoting LGBT rights. Texas, Kansas, Mississippi, and South Dakota are examples of states where more laws restrict LGBT rights. In the majority of US states, LGBT people are not legally protected from discrimination. In 2017 only twenty-two US states had laws against discrimination based on sexual orientation. Only nineteen states had antidiscrimination laws that included sexual orientation and gender identity. Fourteen states protected the rights of LGBT students in the education system. In twenty states, LGBT people were not legally protected from hate crimes.

Since LGBT discrimination may be legal in one state and illegal in another, many LGBT people travel from state to state to find willing officiants and wedding vendors for same-sex weddings, secure jobs with benefits and protection from discrimination, adopt children, or live in a community where they will not face hostility. Summing up written testimonials from one thousand nationwide LGBT readers of the *New York Times*, Frank Bruni observes, "The differences between states—and between cities within states— are profound. . . . Our cities and our states often dictate how easily we can be our true selves at work, buy wedding cakes, construct families—even die."[10] Until there is a comprehensive federal approach to LGBT rights, Americans will continue to receive mixed messages regarding whether—and where—it is against the law to discriminate against LGBT people.

> "The differences between states—and between cities within states—are profound. . . . Our cities and our states often dictate how easily we can be our true selves at work, buy wedding cakes, construct families—even die."[10]
>
> —Frank Bruni, *New York Times* columnist

The Equality Act

A legal solution has been proposed that would make discrimination against LGBT people illegal everywhere in America: the

Equality Act. Senator Jeff Merkley and Representative David Cicilline first proposed the federal Equality Act to Congress in 2015, but in 2018 it had yet to secure enough votes to become a law.

The Equality Act would amend the 1964 Civil Rights Act and other federal nondiscrimination laws to explicitly ban discrimination based on sexual orientation and gender identity. It would prohibit LGBT discrimination in employment, public accommodations (stores, restaurants, hotels, transportation, health care providers), housing, credit, federal jury service, and all federally funded activities, among other areas. Since federal law prevails when federal and state laws disagree, the Equality Act would hold people who discriminate legally accountable for their actions in any US state.

> "Despite significant steps forward, many lesbian, gay, bisexual, transgender, and queer (LGBTQ) Americans continue to lack explicit, uniform protections where they live."[11]
>
> —The Human Rights Campaign

Passing the Equality Act has been a major focus of the LGBT rights movement. The LGBT rights organization the Human Rights Campaign has supported the Equality Act because of the continued prevalence of many types of LGBT discrimination, stating on its website:

Despite significant steps forward, many lesbian, gay, bisexual, transgender, and queer (LGBTQ) Americans continue to lack explicit, uniform protections where they live. 31 states still lack clear, fully-inclusive non-discrimination protections for LGBTQ people, meaning that LGBTQ people are at risk of being fired, denied housing, and denied services for who they are or whom they love.[11]

While the Equality Act would not necessarily prevent discrimination from happening, its supporters have argued that it would send a clear message that anti-LGBT discrimination is against the law—everywhere in America.

CHAPTER 2

LGBT Rights in Public Places

Marriage equality was a major step toward ending LGBT discrimination. Yet LGBT discrimination persists. In fact, organizations such as the ACLU, the National Center for Transgender Equality, and the National LGBTQ Task Force have described a post-gay-marriage backlash in the aftermath of marriage equality in 2015. One of the ways LGBT people experience continuing, and even increased, discrimination is when they are denied rights in public places, including access to public facilities and services.

Denial of Public Services

Many LGBT people report that they are denied services when they attempt to go shopping, eat at restaurants, stay at hotels, seek health care, ride on public transportation, and access a variety of other public services. Transgender people are particularly vulnerable. According to the 2015 US Transgender Survey, almost one-third of transgender people are denied equal service or in some cases physically attacked in public places. The Center for American Progress survey found that 18 percent of LGBT respondents (and 26.7 percent of transgender respondents) said the likelihood of discrimination is a factor that influences where they decide to shop. Among LGBT people who had already experienced discrimination, 33.5 percent avoided public places in general, and 46.9 percent made specific choices about where to shop.

Even in death, LGBT people may experience discrimination in public service. In 2016 the Picayune Funeral Home in Mississippi refused to pick up and cremate the body of Jack Zawadski's husband and partner of fifty-two years, eighty-six-year-old Robert Huskey, when the staff learned that Huskey was gay. "I felt as if the air had been knocked out of me," Zawadski reflected. "Bob was my life, and we had always felt so welcome in this community. And then, at a moment of such personal pain and loss, to have someone do what they did to me, to us, to Bob, I just couldn't believe it."[12] No federal or state law clearly prohibited such discrimination. Zawadski filed a lawsuit in court.

Zawadski's case is an example of how gay and lesbian people ironically became vulnerable to new forms of discrimination when they were granted the legal right to marry. As the Human Rights Campaign's David Stacy observed: "With limited or no federal protections, an LGBT person can get legally married . . . but then be evicted from an apartment and denied a home loan."[13] Many wedding-related and family businesses have refused to serve same-sex partners. These include bakeries, photographers, bed-and-breakfasts, party venues, and adoption agencies. In addition, newly married LGBT people seeking employee benefits for their spouses risk losing a job by outing themselves. In 2016 Emma Green wrote in the *Atlantic*: "The irony of gay marriage becoming legal in the United States is that it has made discrimination against LBGT people easier."[14]

> "With limited or no federal protections, an LGBT person can get legally married . . . but then be evicted from an apartment and denied a home loan."[13]
>
> —David Stacy, the Human Rights Campaign's director of government affairs

The Kim Davis Refusal Case

In a case that attracted national media attention, in 2015 Kentucky county clerk Kim Davis refused to comply with the Supreme Court's decision to legalize same-sex marriage when she turned away same-sex couples applying for marriage licenses. She said that she was acting "under God's authority"[15] because of her religious belief, as an Apostolic Christian, that marriage is limited to unions between a man and a woman. She even went to jail for five days after she defied a federal court order to issue marriage licenses to gay couples.

Ultimately, the governor of Kentucky changed the rules to allow marriage certificates to be printed without the issuing county clerk's name. Same-sex couples were able to procure marriage licenses, and Davis did not have to compromise her religious beliefs by signing them. Davis, therefore, was excused from providing equal

LGBT Life in Mississippi

Mississippi is home to over sixty thousand LGBT adults and the fourteenth-highest percentage of transgender adults in America, according to a 2016 study by the Williams Institute. More LGBT parents are raising children in Mississippi than in any other state in America.

Mississippi-born comedian Tig Notaro, in her semiautobiographical Amazon comedy *One Mississippi* and her 2017 podcast *Out Here in America*, dramatizes her personal experiences of how changing laws affect LGBT people. In 2015 Notaro and her fiancée, Stephanie Allynne, mailed their wedding invitations the day before the Supreme Court legalized gay marriage. After her wedding, Notaro said she felt "joy and pride" to have a marriage certificate from her home state of Mississippi, where same-sex marriage was only recently made legal.

One year later, HB 1523 legalized discrimination against LGBT people in Mississippi. Notaro's joy was tempered by fear for their safety when she and her wife traveled through Mississippi. She realized, while traveling through her home state, that "we could be kicked out of a hotel. We could be kicked out of a restaurant. It was the first time I felt scared."

In her 2017 podcast *Out Here in America*, which explores LGBT life in the Deep South and American heartland, Notaro shares with listeners why marrying in Mississippi was important to her, despite her state's anti-LGBT reputation. She notes the rewards and disappointments and affirms, "I have that hometown pride with the state, and I refuse to leave it behind and discard it."

Quoted in Justin Mitchell, "Tig Notaro Talks About Marriage, LGBT Rights in the Deep South, and *One Mississippi*," *Gulfport (MS) Sun Herald*, June 19, 2017. www.sunherald.com.

treatment to same-sex couples. Several couples sued Davis in court for discrimination on the basis of her original refusal.

The Religious Liberty Debate

Davis's refusal to cooperate with the law because of her religious beliefs was an early episode in what became a central political and legal battle by 2016. This battle revolves around whether religious liberty and First Amendment claims justify her refusal to provide services to LGBT people because of religious beliefs. This issue is at the heart of a polarizing debate between socially conservative proponents of religious liberty and civil rights and non-discrimination advocates.

Behind the argument for a religious liberty exemption are Americans whose religious beliefs include the idea that homo-

Kim Davis, a Kentucky county clerk who refused to issue a marriage license to a same-sex couple, addresses the media. Davis, an Apostolic Christian, said she was acting "under God's authority."

sexuality is a sin or that marriage is only between a man and a woman. They affirm that the government should not force an individual or organization to act against their religious beliefs. For example, the website of the Christian nonprofit group Alliance Defending Freedom expresses the religious liberty view as follows: "Religious freedom is more than allowing diverse religions to co-exist and the opportunity to attend church. It's the ability to act on the convictions of your faith. But today, people of faith are being censored and facing demands to violate their conscience. You should never be forced by the government to act in a way that is morally wrong."[16] This was Davis's position.

In a strongly worded statement, past chair of the US Commission on Civil Rights Martin R. Castro expresses the other side of the debate. He voices his concern that religious liberty cases are really about the right to discriminate rather than the right to preserve freedom. He states: "The phrases 'religious liberty' and 'religious freedom' will stand for nothing except hypocrisy so long as they remain code words for discrimination, intolerance, racism, sexism, homophobia, Islamophobia, Christian supremacy, or any form of intolerance."[17]

Castro's statement is part of the US Commission on Civil Rights 2016 report, released after testimony from experts and scholars about the religious liberty issue. The commission sought to determine whether two American rights—the right to freedom from discrimination and the right to civil liberties including religious freedom—can peacefully coexist in cases for religious liberty exemptions. The commission found that granting religious exemptions to people and organizations that discriminate on the basis of their religious beliefs could greatly infringe on the government's ability to protect civil rights. It recommended that decision makers carefully consider religious liberty cases in which the First Amendment and the Religious Freedom Restoration Act are invoked. Also, the commission advised that courts use a narrow definition of religious exemption while carefully taking into account the specific facts of each case. In response to the report, seventeen religious leaders sent a letter of protest, expressing their opposition to the civil rights position in the ongoing debate.

The First Amendment and Religious Freedom

The two laws invoked to support claims for religious liberty exemptions are the First Amendment and the Religious Freedom Restoration Act. Among other rights, the First Amendment ensures that all Americans may freely exercise their religion. In religious liberty cases, the question is whether freely exercising one's religion provides Americans with the right to discriminate against people whose gender identity or sexual orientation is inconsistent with particular religious beliefs.

The other relevant law, the 1993 Religious Freedom Restoration Act, protects religious individuals from being burdened by the government when they act on their religious beliefs and practices. While the Religious Freedom Restoration Act originally was unrelated to LGBT issues, it became central to efforts to seek religious exemption from claims of discrimination by LGBT people. Between 1993 and March 2017, twenty-one states enacted their own religious freedom restoration acts. In 2015 and 2016 alone, these types of bills were proposed in at least twenty-six states, fueling arguments around LGBT rights.

Among these religious freedom restoration acts that were specifically adapted to LGBT discrimination issues was what the Human Rights Campaign called the most sweeping and devastating anti-LGBT law in America. This was Mississippi's controversial House Bill 1523 (HB 1523), known as the Religious Liberty Accommodations Act, passed into law in 2016. Among other provisions, HB 1523 specifically enabled businesses to refuse to serve LGBT customers and to fire LGBT employees because of their sexual identity or orientation, without legal penalty. HB 1523 also made it legal to force LGBT foster children to submit to conversion therapy and to prohibit transgender children in public schools from wearing clothing that matches their gender identity. A judge blocked the law hours before it was to take effect, but a court of appeals reversed that judge's ruling, and HB 1523 became law. The US Supreme Court declined to hear an appeal in 2018.

LGBT Acceptance by Religious Groups

In light of debates over religious liberty bills, "religious" and "LGBT" are often presented in the media as opposing categories. Many LGBT people report that they feel unwelcome in their religious communities, and some LGBT advocates have experienced serious backlash. For example, James Martin, a Jesuit priest, published a book in 2017 that aimed to build a bridge between the Catholic Church and the LGBT community. Although his book was endorsed by several cardinals and approved by Martin's Jesuit superior, its publication brought Martin insults, threats of violence, social media attacks, and the withdrawal of speaking invitations.

However, acceptance of LGBT people is growing in a number of religions. In a 2014 Pew Research Center survey, the majority of Jews, Catholics, Buddhists, and Hindus, as well as other religious groups, said gay and lesbian sexual orientation should be accepted. Even in religions where a majority of followers do not support LGBT rights, acceptance is growing. A 2017 study by the Pew Research Center found that 52 percent of US Muslims now say that society should accept gay and lesbian sexual orientation, a dramatic 25 percent increase since 2007. Between 2007 and 2014, while support remained low among Mormons, it increased by almost 50 percent (from 24 percent to 35 percent). A growing number of organized religious groups have issued statements welcoming LGBT members, publicly supported LGBT rights issues, ordained LGBT clergy, and included same-sex marriage ceremonies.

The Trump administration has publicly supported religious liberty exemptions from discrimination laws. In 2017 Trump issued an executive order promoting free speech and religious liberty, stating, among other stipulations, that the government should not take action against speech about moral or political issues by religious individuals or organizations. Attorney General Jeff Sessions subsequently released an official government memo that supported the application of the Religious Freedom Restoration Act to justify exemption from penalties for LGBT discrimination. The memo advised federal departments and agencies to increase the weight given to religious liberty claims in discrimination cases. According to the memo, "Except in the narrowest circumstances, no one should be forced to choose between living out his or her faith and complying with the law."[18]

The Wedding Cake Case

The question of how American courts should interpret claims of religious liberty finally reached the Supreme Court in 2017. In December of that year, the court heard arguments in a pivotal case in the battle between religious liberty and gay rights: *Masterpiece Cakeshop v. Colorado Civil Rights Commission*. Five years earlier, in 2012, Jack Phillips of Masterpiece Cakeshop in Lakewood, Colorado, refused to make a wedding cake for David Mullins and Charlie Craig for their upcoming wedding reception. Mullins and Craig planned to marry in Massachusetts and celebrate with a reception in Colorado. The baker told the couple that he could not make a cake for a same-sex wedding. Phillips, who had been in business since 1993 and is a Christian, believes that making a wedding cake for two men would infringe on his freedom of religious expression. Phillips believes that marriage should only take place between a man and a woman.

When Phillips refused to make their wedding cake, Mullins recalls, "we were shocked and mortified and got up and left.

Jack Phillips of Masterpiece Cakeshop refused to make a cake for a same-sex wedding reception. Phillips argued that making a wedding cake for two men would infringe on his freedom of religious expression.

. . . We were embarrassed, and we felt degraded."[19] Since Colorado was one of the twenty states at the time with laws prohibiting discrimination based on sexual orientation, Mullins and Craig were able to file complaints with the Colorado Civil Rights Division. Both the Civil Rights Division and, later, the Colorado Court of Appeals found that Phillips violated the Colorado Anti-Discrimination Act by refusing to bake the cake. These rulings prohibited Phillips from making any wedding cakes until he agreed to stop discriminating against gay customers. Then, attorneys for the Alliance Defending Freedom, the influential conservative Christian nonprofit organization representing Phillips, successfully petitioned the US Supreme Court to hear the case. Numerous amicus curiae, or friend-of-the-court, briefs were filed by LGBT advocates on behalf of the gay couple, and the DOJ filed a brief urging the court to side with the baker.

In his statement to the Supreme Court, Phillips expressed the case for religious freedom: "It's hard to believe that the government is forcing me to choose between providing for my family and employees and violating my relationship with God. That is not freedom. That is not tolerance."[20] Reflecting on the widespread impact of their case, Mullins and Craig stated, "This has always been about more than a cake. Businesses should not be allowed to violate the law and discriminate against us because of who we are and who we love."[21] In June 2018 the Supreme Court decided on the side of the baker, citing anti-religious bias against Phillips by the Colorado Civil Rights Division in the original case. However, the justices postponed for further consideration a broader ruling about whether religious liberty claims entitle other businesses to refuse service to LGBT people.

Bathrooms and Gender Identity

As the *Masterpiece Cakeshop* case worked its way up to the Supreme Court, Americans hotly debated another legal issue involving LGBT public service denial. The most talked-about legal issue around gender identity in the 2010s was transgender bathroom rights.

For many transgender people, the right to access the bathroom of their choice is a matter of dignity, validation, and safety. While some states permit transgender people to use the bathroom of their choice, others do not. Beginning in 2015 several states (including New Hampshire, Colorado, and Texas) debated so-called bathroom bills to restrict transgender bathroom use. According to the *Washington Post*, over one-third of proposed bills to limit LGBT rights in 2016 and 2017 were bathroom bills.

This debate came to a head in 2016, when North Carolina passed the controversial House Bill 2 (HB 2), which banned transgender people from using bathrooms and locker rooms matching their gender identity. In a historic speech, then US attorney general Loretta Lynch declared that HB 2 clearly violated civil rights laws and that the DOJ would file a lawsuit against various parties in North Carolina. Lynch said:

> This action is about a great deal more than just bathrooms. This is about the dignity and respect we accord our fellow citizens and the laws that we, as a people and as a country, have enacted to protect them—indeed, to protect all of us. And it's about the founding ideals that have led this country—haltingly but inexorably—in the direction of fairness, inclusion and equality for all Americans.[22]

In addition to the government lawsuit, HB 2 was met with widespread public and private opposition. Over 180 companies and national leaders boycotted North Carolina because of HB 2. As a result, the state lost major entertainment and sporting events. Among them were a concert by Demi Lovato, the National Basketball Association All-Star Game, and the National Collegiate Athletic Association (NCAA) championship games. The Human Rights Campaign—along with sixty-eight companies that included Apple, Nike, and American Airlines—filed a court brief in support of blocking the law. A study by the Williams Institute predicted that HB 2 could cost North Carolina as much as $5 billion a year (including loss of business investment, tourism, and federal

Gavin Grimm, a transgender high school student, sued the school board for the right to use the boys' bathroom. A federal judge sided with Grimm in May 2018.

funding, as well as costs of litigation and the negative impacts on business productivity, retention, and recruitment).

When North Carolina governor Pat McCrory lost his 2016 re-election campaign, it was widely attributed to his role in supporting HB 2. State legislators repealed the law in 2017 and replaced it with a compromise bill. LGBT advocates, including the ACLU and Lambda Legal, criticized the new bill as a fake repeal, but the NCAA agreed to return its championship games to North Carolina. The DOJ withdrew its HB 2 lawsuit in 2017.

The Gavin Grimm Case

Caught in the changing landscape of the debate over whether transgender rights should be protected is a transgender boy named Gavin Grimm. In 2014 Gavin Grimm was a seventeen-year-old senior at a high school in Gloucester County, Virginia. At first the school principal allowed Grimm to use the boys' bathroom. Then parents complained. After Grimm presented his case to the school board, the school board implemented a policy that all students must use either the bathroom that corresponds with the sex assigned on their birth certificate or a separate single-stall restroom.

Grimm sued the school board for the right to use the boys' bathroom at his high school (under Title IX of the Education Amendments of 1972). After a federal district court dismissed the case in 2015, the US Court of Appeals for the Fourth Circuit ruled in Grimm's favor. Judge Andre Davis wrote in the initial court opinion that Grimm's "case is about much more than bathrooms. It's about a boy asking his school to treat him just like any other boy. It's about protecting the rights of transgender people in public spaces and not forcing them to exist on the margins . . . unrecognized, unrepresented, and unprotected."[23]

The school district appealed, and the Supreme Court agreed to hear the case. But then the Trump administration rescinded Obama-era bathroom guidelines that directed schools to allow transgender students to choose bathrooms matching their gender identity. Citing the change in federal policy, the Supreme Court referred the case back to the lower court for a second hearing. In May 2018 a federal judge in Virginia sided with Grimm. The judge denied the school board's motion to dismiss the case and stated that transgender students are protected under Title IX and the Constitution from exclusionary bathroom policies based on gender identity. Though the ruling is a win for Grimm, it is not necessarily the last word on this topic.

> [Grimm's case is] about a boy asking his school to treat him just like any other boy. It's about protecting the rights of transgender people in public spaces and not forcing them to exist on the margins . . . unrecognized, unrepresented, and unprotected."[23]
>
> —Judge Andre Davis's opinion in the Gavin Grimm case

Beyond Marriage Equality

As the LGBT media watchdog organization GLAAD stated on its website in 2018, "Marriage equality was a milestone, not a finish line."[24] With continued discrimination against LGBT people in public places, high-profile public debates about religious liberty exemptions and transgender bathroom rights, changing federal policies, and pending court decisions, in 2018 many milestones had yet to be reached in the movement for LGBT rights.

CHAPTER 3

Special Issues for LGBT Youth

Adolescence is a turbulent social and emotional period of change. Increasingly, in recent years, it is also when awareness of sexual orientation and gender identity emerges and solidifies for many people. For these youth, LGBT identification is part of a social identity that is still developing. Being LGBT therefore presents special issues for youth.

Today's LGBT Youth

The average age when LGBT people become aware of their sexual orientation and/or gender identity and make it publicly known to others is now much lower than in previous decades. Far more LGBT people now come out to their families and peers during childhood and adolescence. Between 1991 and 2011, the average age for coming out dropped from twenty-five to sixteen, according to a study by Guy Shilo of Israel's Tel Aviv University. More recent research indicates that the average age may now be as low as thirteen, says Caitlin Ryan of San Francisco State University's Family Acceptance Project. The Human Rights Campaign report *Growing Up LGBT in America* indicated that nine of every ten LGBT youth were out to their close friends, and 64 percent were out to their classmates.

It is not necessary to be sexually active in order to identify as gay, lesbian, bisexual, or transgender. Some children know their feelings make them "different" from some of their friends in elementary school or even earlier, and more children now have

Hillside Public Library

the vocabulary to identify that difference as LGBTQ-related. Marisa Calin, author of the young adult novel *Between You & Me*, notes, "The shift I'd like to see more of is the distinction between sexuality defined as who we want to sleep with versus who we love. Prejudiced people make an easy target of 'gay' being about sex, but I noticed the butterflies, the beating heart and the compulsive need to smile long before I had any idea what I wanted to do about it."[25]

One reason for the increasing awareness of LGBT identity among children and youth may be that more information is now available to them. Historian Mark Meinke writes, "Youth today have more options for support than I did. In my youth in a small Midwestern town, there was no support and there were no sources of information. There were no queer-identified places that would reassure me that I was not a hateful anomaly."[26] In contrast, Kate Reese, a thirteen-year-old Nevada girl who began self-identifying as queer in fourth grade, stated in a 2015 interview with BuzzFeed, "I understand what 'queer' means, because all of the information is online. Now I understand LGBT terms, and that it's not a choice. I thought something was wrong with me until I saw all this research. Now I know people like me are out there."[27] In addition to informational resources and social media networks on the Internet, young people today have access to examples of LGBT identity through a significant number of young adult books, television programs, and movies with LGBT characters, as well as popular music and sports figures who are open about being LGBT.

> "In my youth in a small Midwestern town, there was no support and there were no sources of information. There were no queer-identified places that would reassure me that I was not a hateful anomaly."[26]
>
> —Mark Meinke, historian

Increasingly, it is America's youth (and their families) who are dealing with the special issues around first realizing, coming to terms with, and sharing with others an LGBT identity. At the same time, young people must confront all of the other challenges associated with growing up. In school and at home, LGBT youth

Adolescence is a turbulent social and emotional period of change. Increasingly, it is also when awareness of sexual orientation and gender identity emerges for some people.

face challenges and forms of discrimination particular to their age, social and emotional development, and legal status as minors.

Bullying and Harassment at School

Progress in the ongoing effort to improve the experience of LGBT students in school has been slow and uneven. Two major studies recently compared school data over the past ten to fifteen years. One of these is Human Rights Watch's "Like Walking Through a Hailstorm" study, published in 2016. The study's title is borrowed from a metaphor used by a Utah mother to describe the harassment many LGBT children deal with daily in their school hallways. The other study, *From Teasing to Torment: School Climate Revisited*, was published by GLSEN (pronounced "glisten"; originally, Gay, Lesbian & Straight Education Network) in 2015. Both studies found that, despite some improvements in the past decade, LGBT students still face hostile school environments where they are victimized and bullied. They are provided with little protection against

Conversion Therapy for Minors

Alex Cooper's 2016 memoir, *Saving Alex*, recounts how her parents forced her to undergo "conversion therapy" to "cure" her of homosexuality when she was fifteen. Cooper was abused and held prisoner in a Utah home for eight months by unlicensed conversion therapists. After starving herself and attempting suicide, Cooper managed to escape. She went on to win a landmark court case that protected her right to be openly gay as a teenager. In 2018 she was a youth ambassador and LGBT advocate for the Human Rights Campaign.

Conversion therapy presumes that sexual orientation and gender identity is a disorder that can be cured. It has been practiced by health care professionals and spiritual and religious advisers since at least the 1890s. Some conversion therapists use aversion treatments (such as inducing vomiting or using electric shocks) and techniques to suppress homosexual thoughts, including hypnosis. Conversion therapy is widely discredited by medical organizations as unethical and ineffective. Studies show that it often leads to mental health problems and suicide attempts. However, in 2017 forced conversion therapy for minors was only illegal in nine US states (California, Connecticut, Illinois, Nevada, New Jersey, New Mexico, Oregon, Rhode Island, and Vermont) and Washington, DC. According to the think tank Movement Advancement Project, 73 percent of LGBT Americans live in the forty-one states without laws banning conversion therapy for minors. In 2018 the Williams Institute estimated that twenty thousand LGBT youth are likely to be subjected to conversion therapy by a health care provider before age eighteen.

discrimination, and there is inadequate enforcement of antidiscrimination protections where they are in place. For the majority of LGBT youth in America, school remains an unwelcoming place.

Some of the ways LGBT students are bullied at school include biased and homophobic language and taunts, physical and sexual harassment, property damage, cyberbullying, and the spread of rumors and lies. One LGBT youth says, "I want to be able to go to school without being called a faggot or a dyke bitch. I don't want to hide in the shadows about my sexuality because my safety is on the line."[28] The 2015 GLSEN study found that LGBTQ students experienced much higher rates of bias-based bullying than their non-

LGBTQ peers. Over 98 percent said they heard the word *gay* used in a derogatory sense at school, and over 95 percent heard other homophobic remarks about "faggots," "dykes," or "queers." Over 85 percent of LGBT students reported that they were verbally harassed at school, and almost 60 percent were sexually harassed. Close to a third of these students purposely missed school days to avoid being targeted, and 71.5 percent avoided school functions. LGBTQ students also were more likely to be suspended or given detentions.

> "I don't want to hide in the shadows about my sexuality because my safety is on the line."[28]
>
> —Anonymous LGBT youth, quoted in the Human Rights Campaign report

The 2016 Human Rights Watch study similarly found that LGBT students felt unsafe or unwelcome at school because of exclusion, slurs, discouragement of same-sex relationships, and being misgendered by teachers who use the wrong pronouns to describe them. For transgender students, bullying and harassment often takes the form of identity denial. A seventeen-year-old transgender boy from Utah reports, "I've been shoved into lockers, and sometimes people will just push up on me to check if I have boobs."[29] He says that when he complained about this abuse, school administrators blamed him for being open about his gender identity. In fact, many LGBT students do not report bullying and harassment to school authorities because they do not see evidence that help is available.

Consequences of Discrimination

When LGBT youth feel unsafe and victimized at school, and when they lack access to protection, information, and support, they are at high risk for other behaviors and social problems. One LGBT youth states, "It makes me feel afraid to walk around, knowing there are people here in my hometown that hate me, and people like me, enough to attack me."[30] Students who are victimized in school typically have less educational success and are more likely to undergo school discipline. According to the 2015 GLSEN report, LGBT students were three times as likely to say they did not plan to complete high school as their non-LGBT peers. Feeling unsafe or unwelcome in school or at home also has led many LGBT youth to substance abuse, homelessness, mental health issues, and suicide.

Several studies indicate that close to 40 percent of homeless youth in major US cities are LGBT. This figure is especially high, considering that less than 10 percent of the total youth population is LGBT, according to the Williams Institute. Research among LGBT homeless youth shows that most became homeless after being forced out of their home or running away due to family rejection. Further, a 2015 study by the Williams Institute and the True Colors Fund found that LGBT youth tended to be homeless for a longer time period and to report more physical and mental health problems than non-LGBT homeless youth.

Homelessness increases other risks for LGBT youth, including sexual abuse, drug and alcohol addiction, falling behind in (or dropping out of) school, and ultimately failing to find a job. As Jordan Dashow, now a Youth Ambassador for the Human Rights Campaign, explains, being both LGBT and homeless is frightening. He remembers that when he was homeless at age eighteen, "I hid my sexuality just so I would not be bullied or harassed. When I would go to shelters, I was extremely scared that someone would attack me if they found out I was gay."[31]

Family rejection and bullying also greatly increase the risk of depression and suicide for LGBT youth. Numerous studies have shown that transgender youth who are bullied are at especially high risk of attempting suicide. One student from Pennsylvania who attempted suicide at age sixteen remembers hearing harassing comments such as "What is that thing?" when he walked through the hallways of his school. After he came out as transgender, he began skipping school to avoid harassment, and he stopped participating in gendered sports and extracurricular activities. He remembers, "I actually thought I was inhuman. I thought I was an alien. I definitely thought I was going to hell."[32]

School Support for LGBT Education

Schools contribute to serious behavioral risks among LGBT youth when they fail to provide equally supportive learning environments

According to recent reports, only 20 percent of students learned about LGBT history and issues as part of their school curriculum. Some states have laws restricting teachers from discussing LGBT issues at school.

in which to thrive. While there is much more information about LGBT issues available today than in previous decades, it is often not accessible at school. Some schools censor or limit access to LGBT resources and information via computers, the Internet, and library collections. For example, while an increasing number of young adult books have featured LGBT main characters and topics since 2013, these LGBT titles were at the top of the American Library Association's list of books that were challenged or banned in 2016 and 2017.

LGBT educational equality would mean that all students would learn about important LGBT historical figures and topics in school. According to the GLSEN report, only 20 percent of students learned about LGBT history and issues as part of their school curriculum. In seven states (Alabama, Arizona, Louisiana, Mississippi, Oklahoma, South Carolina, and Texas), laws restrict teachers and counselors from talking or teaching about LGBT issues at school (including health counseling). Restrictions in these and other states prevent LGBT youth from obtaining equal access to information about health and well-being. For example, a seventeen-year-old boy in Utah reports, "In my health class I tested the water by asking [the teacher] about safer sex, because I'm gay. He said he was not allowed to talk about it."[33]

Some efforts to include LGBT issues in school curricula have been made, although not without controversy. In 2015 the school board in Fairfax County, Virginia, the largest public school system in the state, approved the inclusion of LGBT information in its public school sex education curriculum. The changes were met with intense opposition from parents who attended a school board meeting on the issue. In 2011 California passed the country's first law requiring public schools to feature LGBT-inclusive content in its history curriculum, the FAIR Education Act. In 2017 the California State Board of Education approved the first LGBT-inclusive textbooks. These textbooks contain specific references to historical figures who were LGBT or who had disabilities. It remains to be seen whether other states will follow suit.

> "In my health class I tested the water by asking [the teacher] about safer sex, because I'm gay. He said he was not allowed to talk about it."[33]
>
> —A seventeen-year-old boy in Utah

Finally, LGBT students need more support and antidiscrimination intervention from teachers and staff. According to the 2015 GLSEN report, almost six in ten LGBT students were provided with no protection from bullying at their schools. While teachers increasingly felt they should do something to support LGBT students, half of the teachers reported that they did not intervene in bullying or provide support. Teachers specifically identified the need for training in effective intervention strategies for how to handle these situations.

The Safe Schools Movement

The safe schools movement emerged in the 1990s to fight for educational equality and an end to discrimination against LGBT students and to provide needed resources for students and teachers. One of the most important outcomes of the safe

Homecoming Queens

In the 2010s students at several American high schools challenged gender norms by electing gender-nonconforming LGBT students as homecoming kings and queens—with mixed response. In 2011 Rebeca Arellano was crowned as the first female homecoming king at San Diego's Patrick Henry High School. Arellano's girlfriend, Haileigh Adams, was crowned as queen. "We have a lot of support, but there are also a lot of people who are angry about it," Adams told ABC News. "Anonymous Patrick Henry students are saying they're embarrassed and that it's wrong for a girl to take the spot of king. But . . . it's not really fair for us not to have the right to run as a couple."

Transgender student Cassidy Lynn Campbell was elected homecoming queen at Marina High School in Huntington Beach, California, in 2013. Some students responded with hurtful comments. On the evening of her election Campbell posted a video on her YouTube channel in which she broke down in tears while explaining her feelings about the backlash. "After 16 years of struggling, I finally do it and I finally am myself—thinking I'll be so happy," she said. "It's just sad that everyone has to be so judgmental about it, and so hateful, and so mean and so negative." Subsequent high school transgender homecoming queens have reported similar bittersweet mixtures of gratifying support and discriminatory comments.

Quoted in Olivia Katrandjian, "Lesbian Student Named Homecoming King at High School in San Diego," ABC News, October 29, 2011. http://abcnews.go.com.

Quoted in Cavan Sieczkowski, "Cassidy Lynn Campbell, Transgender Teen, Named Homecoming Queen," *Huffington Post*, September 21, 2013. www.huffingtonpost.com.

schools movement has been the emergence of numerous gay-straight alliances at schools. These groups are made up of students, teachers, and staff who work together to transform the school environment and promote inclusivity. They provide services and activities to make schools safer and more welcoming for LGBT youth and to provide them with a voice. For example, gay-straight alliances have promoted appropriate responses to anti-LGBT incidents at schools, and they have advocated for programs that educate students and faculty about ways to prevent discrimination. However, LGBT students report that some schools have blocked or restricted the formation of these groups.

Students blow bubbles during a gay-straight alliance event. Gay-straight alliances at schools have formed to end discrimination against and abuse of LGBT students and to provide a safe school environment.

Another outcome of the safe schools movement is the push for the federal Safe Schools Improvement Act. Several studies have shown that LGBT students experience less bullying and discrimination in schools that have antibullying policies. The Safe Schools Improvement Act would mandate that every public K–12 school in America implement an antibullying policy that includes specific provisions for sexual orientation and gender identity. This act has been introduced in both the Senate and the House of Representatives. It has not yet gained enough votes to be passed as a law.

Since studies agree that more and more young people are identifying and coming out as LGBT, the safe schools movement is increasingly relevant in the twenty-first century. Its leaders continue to spearhead efforts to address the special issues faced by LGBT youth, including bullying and harassment, high rates of homelessness, rejection by family and friends, and limited access to LGBT information and resources.

CHAPTER 4

Discrimination in Employment and the Workplace

Many LGBT people feel that they cannot be themselves at work because of discrimination. They keep their LGBT status secret and lie about their personal lives at work and job interviews. They fear that they will lose their jobs if their LGBT identity becomes known.

Over half of LGBT employees said discrimination negatively impacted their work environment, according to the Center for American Progress survey. For example, one woman who lives in North Carolina reported that she commutes a long distance to her job so she can live in a town where LGBT people feel welcomed. She loves her job, but she remains in the closet at work. She worries that her supervisors might fire her if they knew about her sexuality. Another example is a gay man who works at a Fortune 500 company and makes sure there is nothing in his demeanor to suggest to colleagues or clients that he is gay. He explains, "I'm trying to minimize the bias against me by changing my presentation in the corporate world. I lower my voice in meetings to make it sound less feminine and avoid wearing anything but a black suit."[34]

These are realistic concerns. In all but twenty-two US states and Washington, DC, no laws clearly protect LGBT people from discrimination in employment or the workplace.

Many States Do Not Protect LGBT Workers from Discrimination

In 2018 twenty-eight states had no statewide laws that clearly protect LGBT people from discrimination in employment or the workplace. According to Movement Advancement Project, one of every two LGBT people in America lives in a state with no legal protection against employment discrimination based on gender identity and sexual orientation.

Employment nondiscrimination law covers sexual orientation and gender identity *(20 states + DC)*	Employment nondiscrimination law covers only sexual orientation, though federal law offers some protections *(2 states)*	No employment nondiscrimination law covering sexual orientation or gender identity, though federal law offers some protections *(28 states)*	State has law preventing passage or enforcement of local non-discrimination laws

Source: Movement Advancement Project Equality Maps. "Non-Discrimination Laws," March 29, 2018. www.lgbtmap.org.

About one in four LGBT people experienced discrimination in 2016, according to the Center for American Progress. Workers who are openly LGBT are much more likely to face discrimination. In some cases employment discrimination may lead to psychological distress, physical health problems, low job satisfaction, failure to show up for work, increased likelihood of quitting a needed job, and in some cases poverty, homelessness, and food insecurity.

Hiring Bias

Many LGBT people face discrimination from the start of the employment process, when they apply for a job. When two equally qualified candidates apply for a job, studies have shown that a known or suspected LGBT candidate is less likely to be hired. These studies, conducted in 2011 and 2016 and published in the *American Journal of Sociology* and *Socius*, submitted sets of fake résumés for two different candidates with equivalent qualifications as applications for real jobs. One résumé in each set included references to LGBT identity (such as serving in a leadership role for a campus LGBT organization). The results showed that gay men were about 40 percent less likely to be interviewed than straight men, and women whose résumés included LGBT references were 30 percent less likely to be called back for an interview than other women. LGBT people of color are impacted at even higher levels by bias in the hiring process. It is not surprising, then, that 12 percent of LGBT people of color (and 18.7 percent of LGBT job seekers aged eighteen to twenty-four) removed items from their résumés that might out them as LGBT, according to the Center for American Progress report.

Some employers knowingly discriminate against LGBT candidates, especially in US states where hiring discrimination is not explicitly illegal. However, even employers who try not to discriminate may have unconscious hiring biases. An Italian study published in *Archives of Sexual Behavior* in 2017 found that when heterosexual listeners perceived men and women's voices as "sounding gay," they were less likely to identify those individuals as suitable for a professional leadership position and high salary range. Some businesses are exploring how to use technology to avoid the influence of unconscious bias in hiring decisions.

Bullying, Harassment, and Exclusion at Work

Many LGBT employees who successfully complete the hiring process and find gainful employment confront high levels of bullying, harassment, and exclusion at work. In 2017 a nationwide survey by Harris Poll for CareerBuilder found that 40 percent of LGBT employees had been bullied at work. Over half of those who were bullied said the behavior occurred repeatedly. Some LGBT employees report that coworkers make false accusations about them or refuse to acknowledge them when they speak. Others find that people at work pick on their appearance or mannerisms, or make belittling and critical comments, including name-calling and homophobic language or jokes. Some LGBT people reveal that coworkers criticize them for not looking feminine or masculine enough or say that they do not have "real" marriages. Almost one in five LGBT workers who reported bullying say they suffered from health problems related to the experience. More than two in five left a job because of bullying.

Being bullied and harassed at work is especially common for transgender employees. In a Movement Advancement Project study, 78 percent of transgender employees reported being harassed at work. For example, transgender employees were forced to use bathrooms or dress in ways that do not match their gender identity. They also stated that private information was shared with coworkers about their transgender status without their permission. The National Center for Transgender Equality found in 2016 that 30 percent of employed transgender respondents were fired, denied a promotion, or mistreated in some way by their employers. As a result of their work environment, 77 percent kept their transgender identity secret, delayed a gender transition, or quit a job.

Some LGBT workers say that exclusion from social circles and gatherings related to career advancement is a subtle but powerful form of workplace discrimination. For example, a Fortune 500 company employee says his workplace has a nondiscrimination policy that prevents him from being fired for being gay. However, he finds that he is often excluded from important social career opportunities. He explains, "When partners at the firm invite straight men to squash or drinks, they don't invite the women or gay men. I'm passed over for opportunities that could lead to being pro-

Two LGBT Military Pioneers

The repeal of Don't Ask, Don't Tell resulted in part from the efforts of military personnel who came out as LGBT and fought discrimination. Leonard Matlovich served in the Vietnam War and was honored with a Purple Heart, the Bronze Star, and two US Air Force commendations for bravery. He was discharged in 1975 after he became the first US military service member to come out as gay while serving. He spent the rest of his life working to end the military's LGBT employment ban. He was featured on the cover of *Time* magazine for his activism. Today gay rights groups organize demonstrations and Veterans Day celebrations at his Washington, DC, grave site. His gravestone inscription reads, "A Gay Vietnam Veteran: When I was in the military they gave me a medal for killing two men—and a discharge for loving one."

Eric Alva later helped transform the image of LGBT people in the military when he came out publicly as gay in 2006. As the first American service member seriously wounded in the 2003 Iraq War, Alva had been honored with a Purple Heart and a visit from President George W. Bush. He had been portrayed in the media as a war hero. Alva's public announcement helped transform the image of LGBT military personnel from "deviant" to "normal." After Alva, other Iraq veterans came out as LGBT. By 2010, when the Military Readiness Enhancement Act repealed Don't Ask, Don't Tell, polls indicated that most Americans favored allowing LGBT military service.

Quoted in Steve Estes, "LGBTQ Military Service," in *LGBTQ America: A Theme Study of Lesbian, Gay, Bisexual, Transgender, and Queer History*, ed. Megan E. Springate. Washington, DC: National Park Foundation, 2016. www.nps.gov.

moted."[35] These exclusions are all the more important in light of the Center for American Progress report finding that from 11 percent to 28 percent of LGBT workers lost a promotion because of their sexual orientation.

Unequal Pay and Benefits

Another form of unequal treatment that LGBT people face at work is lower pay and benefits. LGBT workers earn less on average than non-LGBT workers, and this contributes to higher rates of poverty, unemployment, and homelessness. According to the

National Transgender Discrimination Survey, transgender people are almost four times as likely as the general population to earn under $10,000 a year, even though most are college educated.

In addition to the LGBT wage gap, companies that provide health insurance and benefits to heterosexual partners do not always extend this coverage to same-sex partners and/or spouses. Even companies that are considered LGBT-friendly may have policies that keep their workplaces from being truly discrimination-free. For example, in 2017 transgender Starbucks supervisor Niko Walker discovered that the company's paid family leave policy for retail store employees disproportionately benefits birth mothers over LGBT parents, who are more likely to be raising adopted and foster children. Mothers who work in Starbucks stores and give birth to a child received six weeks of paid leave. Fathers and adoptive parents were ineligible for paid leave after the birth of a child.

A gay couple holds their newly adopted baby girl. Paid family leave benefits offered by companies often disproportionately benefit birth mothers over LGBT parents.

Walker started an online petition to ask Starbucks to increase leave time for LGBTQ families. The petition went viral, attracting twenty thousand signatures in just a few days. Starbucks management agreed to examine its policies, and in 2018 Starbucks announced a new policy that extends six weeks of paid parental leave to all new parents.

This is a success story for LGBT workplace equality. Walker publicly noted Starbucks' responsiveness to employee concerns, and he praised Starbucks for the support he received while transitioning from female to male as a barista. At many other companies, employees are less optimistic about the results of speaking up about discriminatory policies.

Firing and Job Security

More unsettling than the problem of lower pay and benefits for many working LGBT people is knowing that they could lose their jobs if their employers become aware of their sexual orientation and/or gender identity. Eighty-seven percent of Americans believe that it is illegal in the United States to fire someone because they are LGBT, according to the Movement Advancement Project, but this is not true. Presidents Bill Clinton and Barack Obama both issued executive orders that increased protections of LGBT federal employees, and many companies have their own internal nondiscrimination policies. However, no clear federal law prohibits firing people because of their LGBT status.

The Employment Non-Discrimination Act (ENDA) was first introduced in Congress in 1994 and was reintroduced nearly every subsequent year. The Senate passed the bill in 2013, but it never received enough support in the House and therefore did not become law. ENDA aimed to prohibit LGBT workplace harassment and discrimination based on sexual orientation and gender identity in hiring, promotion, and firing. In 2015 ENDA's provisions were absorbed into the broader proposed Equality Act, which has yet to be passed.

Precedent-Setting Employment Cases

While no federal law protects employees from losing their jobs because of their sexual orientation or gender identity, some Americans who were fired after making their LGBT identity known have brought precedent-setting cases to US courts. Kimberly Hively went to court in 2014 after her teaching contract was not renewed and she was denied a permanent full-time teaching job by her employer. Hively had worked for fourteen years as an adjunct math professor at Ivy Tech Community College in South Bend, Indiana. After her employers learned that she was a lesbian, her employment was terminated. According to Hively, the trouble started when she gave her girlfriend a quick good-bye kiss in the car. Hively later told CNN, "It was just a kiss in the car like millions of other people do." She received a phone call about her professionalism from her school administration, apparently responding to a complaint that she was "sucking face."[36]

After Hively's initial case was dismissed by a lower court, she appealed, represented by the national LGBT civil rights legal organization Lambda Legal. In 2017 the US Court of Appeals for the Seventh Circuit gave Hively the green light to go back to the lower court and sue the college. This was the first time a US appellate court had ruled that sexual orientation may be protected under Title VII of the Civil Rights Act. Hively, who became a high school math teacher, says, "I'm hoping . . . it'll close the gap that was left when the marriage law passed and there was no protection outside of the ability to get married."[37]

By favoring a reading of Title VII of the Civil Rights Act that includes protections for sexual orientation, the *Hively* ruling paved the way for the landmark case of Donald Zarda. Zarda loved extreme sports and worked as a skydiving instructor for Altitude Express in Long Island, New York. One day in 2010, when a female student seemed uncomfortable about having her body strapped tightly to Zarda's for a tandem skydiving jump, Zarda revealed that he was gay. Court transcripts indicate that he often told female students about his sexual orientation so they would not feel awk-

Corporate Equality

The Human Rights Campaign's Corporate Equality Index provides an indicator of the increasing number of businesses that promote LGBTQ equality in the twenty-first century. The index rates a wide range of American companies, large and small and public and private. Top-rated companies have nondiscrimination policies, equitable benefits, internal education to promote LGBTQ inclusion, and a public commitment to LGBTQ equality. When the index rating process first began in 2002, only 13 companies merited a top rating of 100 percent as Best Places to Work for LGBTQ Equality. In 2018 the top rating was earned by 609 businesses in a variety of industries across America. The most striking development in businesses that earned the title of 2018 Best Places to Work for LGBTQ Equality was their increased adoption of transgender-inclusive initiatives.

ward about close bodily contact with him. This time, however, the student's boyfriend complained to Zarda's boss, who fired Zarda.

Zarda dreamed of becoming a pilot, and he feared that having been fired would make it difficult for him to find another job. He filed a lawsuit against Altitude Express. In the lawsuit, Zarda claimed that the company discriminated against him because of his sexual orientation, thereby violating Title VII of the 1964 Civil Rights Act. Since the Civil Rights Act explicitly protects people from discrimination based on sex, the case hinged on the question of whether sex should be understood to mean sexual orientation.

Zarda lost his case in federal district court and again with his first appeal. When the case was heard in the US Court of Appeals for the Second Circuit in 2018, two federal agencies weighed in on both sides of the case. The EEOC stated that sexual orientation should be protected. The DOJ filed an amicus brief arguing that sex discrimination only applies to differential treatment of men versus women. In a historic decision, the court ruled in Zarda's favor, joining the US Court of Appeals for the Seventh Circuit as another federal court to recognize LGBT as a protected category.

Zarda did not live to celebrate the decision. In 2014 he died on an extreme BASE jumping trip in Europe. His sister and his partner, William Allen Moore, continued Zarda's case for him as coexecutors of his estate. After the court ruling, Moore reflected, "I wish he [Zarda] could have been here, because he never would have thought it would get this far. He would have been so happy and elated that he changed this for LGBT people."[38]

In March 2018 the US Court of Appeals for the Sixth Circuit expanded on these cases about the inclusion of sexual orientation as a protected category. It ruled that discrimination based on transgender status also is a form of sex discrimination. Transgender funeral director Aimee Stephens had been fired two weeks after she told her Michigan funeral home employer that she planned to transition from male to female. The funeral home owner, Thomas Rost, argued that he should not be forced to employ a transgender worker due to his Christian religious beliefs that "a person's sex (whether male or female) is an immutable God-given gift and that people should not deny or attempt to change their sex."[39] After Stephens filed a complaint, the EEOC represented her in court in this important case for transgender equality.

> "A person's sex (whether male or female) is an immutable God-given gift . . . people should not deny or attempt to change their sex."[39]
>
> —Thomas Rost, defendant in transgender employment discrimination lawsuit

Businesses Taking the Lead

While courts wrestle with legal arguments about employment discrimination, a growing number of businesses promote and support LGBT employment rights by implementing internal policies. According to the Human Rights Campaign, over 82 percent of Fortune 500 companies in the United States now offer such policies. These policies include equal treatment for LGBT people in hiring, benefits, promotion, and other areas; providing health insurance to same-sex partners and supporting gender-affirmation surgery for transgender employees; educating employees about using the correct pronoun when addressing transgender employees; and more.

Also, in recent years, businesses have made public statements supporting LGBT equality. For example, 379 businesses and business organizations filed an amicus brief to support four marriage equality cases in 2015. The brief stated that laws restricting LGBT marriage limit companies' ability to attract and retain top employees. Angie's List and Twitter protested Indiana's religious freedom law in 2015 by canceling and/or halting planned programs. Numerous companies led or joined boycotts of North Carolina after that state passed its controversial law restricting transgender bathroom use.

> "If hearing that the CEO of Apple is gay can help someone struggling to come to terms with who he or she is, or bring comfort to anyone who feels alone, or inspire people to insist on their equality, then it's worth the tradeoff with my own privacy."[40]
>
> —Tim Cook, CEO of Apple

Business leaders who identify as LGBT also serve as role models when they come out publicly. In 2014 Tim Cook of Apple became the first openly gay chief executive officer (CEO) of a Fortune 500 company. He wrote in *Bloomberg Businessweek*, "If hearing that the CEO of Apple is gay can help someone struggling to come to terms with who he or she is, or bring comfort to anyone who feels alone, or inspire people to insist on their equality, then it's worth the tradeoff with my own privacy."[40]

LGBT Employees in the Military

Military service is a specialized type of employment in which LGBT people have long faced discrimination and harassment. LGBT people have served secretly in the US military since the time of the Revolutionary War. When the LGBT status of military personnel became publicly known, typically they were punished and/or discharged (usually dishonorably). According to historian Allan Bérubé, the military discharged almost one hundred thousand personnel between 1943 and 1993 for alleged homosexuality. A particularly dramatic example took place during the Cold War in the 1950s, when the US government fired around five thousand gay and lesbian military employees and civilian defense workers. LGBT people were said to be a security threat and easier targets for blackmail by Communist agents.

In 1993 President Bill Clinton implemented the Don't Ask, Don't Tell policy. The policy prohibited inquiries regarding the LGBT status of military employees. However, the basic policy remained; known LGBT status was considered incompatible with military service, and military personnel still risked discharge if their identity became public. Many LGBT people who were victims of harassment and violence by supervisors or fellow military personnel were afraid to speak out for fear they would out themselves and be discharged or punished. This created an unsafe situation.

In 2010 President Obama signed the Military Readiness Enhancement Act into law. The act repealed Don't Ask, Don't Tell and outlawed discrimination against LGB people (but not transgender people) in military employment. The repeal of Don't Ask, Don't Tell was made possible in part by government studies regarding the costs of its implementation and the readiness of LGB people to serve in the military. A study by the Williams Institute estimated that about seventy-one thousand gay, lesbian, and/or bisexual men and women already served in the military in 2010 (about 2.2 percent of all military personnel). Under the Military Readiness Enhancement Act, LGB people were able to serve openly beginning in 2011. Further, veterans who were discharged because of their sexual orientation could now request that their discharge status be changed from dishonorable to honorable.

For the estimated 15,500 transgender people currently serving in the military, changing federal policies have resulted in uncertainty. A 2016 Rand Corporation study commissioned by the US military concluded that allowing transgender military personnel to serve would at most have a minimal impact on military readiness, military health care costs, unit cohesiveness, and the effectiveness of operations. In June 2016 Secretary of Defense Ash Carter of-

A military member marches in an LGBT Pride parade in 2012. In 2010 President Obama repealed "Don't Ask, Don't Tell" and outlawed discrimination against LGB people (excludes transgender) in the military.

ficially ended the ban on transgender military service. However, in July 2017, Trump issued a statement via Twitter repealing the right of transgender people to serve in the military. The president wrote, "The United States government will not accept or allow . . . Transgender individuals to serve in any capacity in the U.S. military. Our military must be focused on decisive and overwhelming . . . victory and cannot be burdened with the tremendous medical costs and disruption that transgender in the military would entail."[41]

Federal courts blocked the immediate implementation of Trump's transgender military ban. Civil rights groups also filed lawsuits on behalf of transgender personnel already serving in the military. In February 2018, with Trump's transgender ban stalled in the courts, the first openly transgender recruit signed a contract

"Today, it's possible for a lesbian couple to get legally married on Saturday and then be fired on Monday for putting a wedding picture on their desk."[42]

—Selisse Berry, founder and CEO at Out & Equal Workplace Advocates

with the US military. Then in March 2018 Trump approved a policy that banned transgender people who have had or require gender transition (a process that may include both hormone-replacement therapy and gender-affirmation surgery) from military service. The new policy enables the Pentagon to make exceptions as needed, echoing the approach of Don't Ask, Don't Tell. Transgender advocates plan to fight the new transgender service policy in court. As the debate unfolds, the employment security of transgender people in the military remains in jeopardy.

The Safety of the Closet

For LGBT employees, the cost of making their sexual orientation or gender identity known can be severe. Selisse Berry, founder and CEO at Out & Equal Workplace Advocates, notes that even though LGBT people may now legally marry, they still have good reason to remain in the closet at work. Berry observes, "Today, it's possible for a lesbian couple to get legally married on Saturday and then be fired on Monday for putting a wedding picture on their desk."[42] Efforts to end LGBT discrimination in employment—including the Equality Act, landmark court cases, and the ground-level work of employees and employers across America—are under way. In the meantime, many of America's LGBT workers keep their identity secret in order to protect their jobs and their well-being.

CHAPTER 5

Violence Against LGBT People

Pulse nightclub was known as a place where the Orlando, Florida, gay community—especially those of Latino descent—gathered to dance and socialize. In June 2016 Pulse became the scene of what was, at the time, the deadliest mass shooting in both US history and LGBT history. The shooter, twenty-nine-year-old Omar Mateen, reportedly became angry when he saw two men kissing. He then researched gay nightclubs in Orlando. In the early morning of June 12, 2016, during Gay Pride Month, Mateen entered Pulse nightclub. He shot and murdered forty-nine people and wounded fifty-three others before he was killed by law enforcement. During the shooting, many people who were trapped inside the club called 911 and sent terrified text messages to their families and friends. Eddie Justice, who was among those who lost their lives at Pulse, texted his mother, "Mommy I love you. . . . I'm gonna die."[43] Those who survived continue to suffer from the after effects of trauma, as do the families and friends of the victims and survivors.

The Pulse nightclub shooting was not the first or the last time that LGBT people were targets of violence in a location they considered to be a safe gathering place. The renowned Stonewall riots, considered the beginning of the gay rights movement in 1969, started at a New York City gay nightclub when LGBT people fought back against a police raid. In the largest mass killing of LGBT people before the Pulse shooting,

Family and friends support each other after a deadly shooting at a gay nightclub in Orlando, Florida. The shooter, who was targeting gay men, killed forty-nine people and injured fifty-three others before he was killed by police.

arson left thirty-two people dead in the gay bar UpStairs Lounge in New Orleans in 1973. No one was charged with the crime, and some dead bodies went unclaimed because families refused to identify their LGBT children. On New Year's Eve 2013, 750 people escaped with their lives after a fire was set in the stairwell at a Seattle gay club called Neighbours. Shortly after the Pulse shooting, a man was arrested who was apparently heading to the Los Angeles Gay Pride Parade with explosives.

As a deadly episode in this history of attacks on gay "safe" spaces, the Pulse nightclub shooting motivated crowds to attend numerous vigils, rallies, and protests in 2016. It also sparked a national discussion about the nature and prevalence of hate crimes and the urgency of addressing violence against LGBT people in America.

What Is a Hate Crime?

A hate crime occurs when an illegal act (such as arson, murder, assault, or vandalism) is committed with a motive of bias. If the Pulse nightclub shooting had taken place before 2009, it would not have been investigated by local and federal law enforcement authorities as a hate crime against LGBT people. Before 2009 hate crime status was limited to criminal acts motivated by bias against the victim's race, color, religion, or national origin. Violent crimes based on gender, gender identity, sexual orientation, and disability became classified as federal hate crimes after Obama signed the Matthew Shepard and James Byrd Jr. Hate Crimes Prevention Act into law in 2009.

The Hate Crimes Prevention Act is considered to be the first major federal gay rights law in America. The law was named after two victims of violent crimes. Matthew Shepard was a gay twenty-one-year-old college student who was brutally beaten and left in a field to die by two assailants in 1998 in Laramie, Wyoming. James Byrd Jr. was an African American man who was dragged to his death that same year. Public outcry over the gruesome and violent circumstances of these tragic deaths led to the movement to expand federal hate crime protections, resulting in the 2009 Hate Crimes Prevention Act. In 2013, despite opposition from Republican legislators, Congress provided further protections based on sexual orientation and gender identity when it reauthorized the Violence Against Women Act.

Statistics and Reporting of Anti-LGBT Violence

The Hate Crimes Prevention Act requires collection of data about bias-motivated crimes in the United States each year. The DOJ obtains information about crimes motivated by prejudice from US law enforcement agencies. LGBT rights organizations such as the Human Rights Campaign, Southern Poverty Law Center, and National Coalition of Anti-Violence Programs (NCAVP) also collect and/or analyze data about violence against LGBT people and advocate for solutions.

Several LGBT rights organizations suggest that violent acts against LGBT individuals have long been underreported. Many LGBT victims are afraid of outing themselves to family, employers, or friends by making an official report. Also, many survivors of anti-LGBT violence are reluctant to report offenses to the police. In 2016 LGBT victims said police officers were actually the perpetrators of 10 percent of the 1,036 anti-LGBT violent crimes reported to the NCAVP by organizations around the country. Further, in about a third of the cases in which survivors of anti-LGBT hate crimes interacted with police in 2016, police officers were reportedly hostile or indifferent. Survivors of hate crimes also report police misconduct at the scene of a crime, including excessive force and unjustified arrests. When LGBT people do make reports, the NCAVP finds that some police may not classify bias-motivated violence against LGBT people as hate crimes. While many law enforcement officials follow up on hate crimes and respond appropriately, those who do not do so contribute to underreporting.

A woman reports a crime at a police station. Many violent acts targeting LGBT individuals go unreported as the victims are afraid of outing themselves to friends, family, and employers by making an official report.

In recent years statistics show that anti-LGBT violence has increased. It is difficult to know whether these numbers reflect more actual incidents or more reporting by LGBT crime victims. Due to underreporting, violence and hate crimes against LGBT people may be even more prevalent than available data suggest.

Prevalence

LGBT people are frequent targets of violent crimes. According to FBI data, in 2014 LGBT people became the minority group most targeted by hate crimes, representing almost 20 percent of the 5,462 single-bias hate crimes reported to the FBI that year. In 2016 the Southern Poverty Law Center analyzed fourteen years of FBI hate crime data and found that LGBT people were targeted more than other minority groups in America during that period. LGBT hate crimes occurred at a rate that was twice as high as crimes directed at Muslims or African Americans, four times as high as Jews, and fourteen times as high as Latinos.

A disturbing spike in reported anti-LGBT violence, especially against LGBT people of color, began in 2015 and escalated in 2016. According to the NCAVP, in over half of reported hate-related violence in 2016, the victim knew the perpetrator. LGBT people were especially victimized by their landlords, neighbors, family members, and employers. Some of these incidents involved physical attacks. Others involved verbal harassment, threats, and intimidation. One in three survivors were physically injured as a result of anti-LGBT violence in 2016.

LGBT homicides sharply increased in 2016. In addition to the forty-nine people who died at Pulse nightclub, there were twenty-eight bias-motivated killings of LGBT people in 2016, up from twenty-four in 2015. All told, the number of LGBT people killed in 2016 exceeded the number of known LGBT murders in the past twenty years.

This trend continued in 2017. A special midyear report by the NCAVP called *A Crisis of Hate* documented thirty-six hate-related LGBT murders, an average of about one homicide a week, in the first eight months of 2017. Three out of four of these LGBT victims were people of color. Among other homicides, a transgender sixteen-year-old was shot to death and covered with bleach in an Iowa alley. A Los Angeles man was convicted of murdering his own son; according to court witnesses, the man was disgusted by his son's sexual orientation.

There has been an especially dramatic increase in the number of transgender murders. In 2015, according to the Human Rights Campaign, more transgender people were killed than in any past year on record. Most of these transgender homicide victims were people of color. In each subsequent year, murders of transgender women of color rose.

Explaining Increased Violence

LGBT rights organizations and leaders have proposed theories to explain the increase in violence and hate crimes against LGBT people in recent years. One possibility is that growing public acceptance of LGBT people by most Americans, along with marriage equality and other new protections, has radicalized and threatened LGBT opponents and led them to criminal behavior. Psychologist and antigay violence expert Gregory M. Herek supports this view. He affirms that people who oppose marriage equality "may feel that the way they see the world is threatened, which motivates them to strike out in some way, and for some people, that way could be in violent attacks."[44]

Several organizations and movement leaders suggest that the divisive political climate surrounding the transition from President Obama to President Trump and the controversies over bathroom bills also may have led to increased violence. In 2016 LGBT issues were highly visible in the media. Numerous bills to limit LGBT rights were introduced, and transgender bathroom access was hotly debated as a result of North Carolina's controversial HB 2

Platform to End Violence Against LGBT Communities

The NCAVP's 2017 *Platform to End Violence Against LGBT Communities* recommends six calls to action to end LGBT violence, paraphrased here:

- Recognize historical systems of oppression and incorporate anti-oppression work in all efforts to end violence.
- Support community-based efforts for healing and survivor justice.
- Advocate for opportunities that affirm the experiences of transgender and gender nonconforming people of color.
- Call out and resist religious exemption and public accommodation bills and advocate for increased legal LGBT protection.
- Act in solidarity with movements supporting people impacted by oppression and violence.
- Actively work to create a culture that nurtures LGBTQ youth by uplifting the experiences of LGBTQ communities.

law and Gavin Grimm's deferred Supreme Court case. In its 2016 report, the NCAVP stated:

> If 2016 has shown us anything it's that the LGBTQ community is resilient and committed to ending violence against all communities. In the year ahead as we continue to resist anti-LGBTQ violence, roll backs of LGBTQ rights, and work in solidarity with movements seeking liberation, may we remember those we have lost in 2016, and organize and advocate for those still living at the margins.[45]

Effects of Violence on the LGBT Community

The effects of anti-LGBT violence and hate crimes often linger as depression, anxiety, anger, and fear. According to a study

"Hate crimes have a devastating effect beyond the harm inflicted on any one victim. They reverberate through families, communities, and the entire nation."[46]

—The DOJ

published in the *Journal of Homosexuality*, these negative effects are felt by victims much longer than the effects of attacks that are not linked with bias. Often, these negative ramifications are felt not only by the victims but also by the larger LGBT community, whose members feel targeted by extension. The DOJ website affirms the widespread impact and extensive social harm of hate crimes: "Hate crimes have a devastating effect beyond the harm inflicted on any one victim. They reverberate through families, communities, and the entire nation, as others fear that they too could be threatened, attacked, or forced from their homes, because of what they look like, who they are, where they worship, whom they love, or whether they have a disability."[46]

Because many anti-LGBT crimes are committed in places that should be safe—such as home, work, or school—victims also continue to fear afterward for their physical and psychological safety. Further, because of the prevalence of anti-LGBT violence in certain geographical places or institutions, LGBT people who have not yet experienced violence themselves may alter their behavior to avoid violence. Neighborhoods, places of employment, public transportation, and nightclubs are examples of the types of places that may be viewed as sites of possible violence. For example, a gay man in California reported to the Center for American Progress that he chose to apply only to law schools in cities that he considered safe for an LGBT man of color, thus limiting his future career options. A gay father from South Carolina reported to the *New York Times*, "Somebody said that our kids should be taken away from us

"Somebody said that our kids should be taken away from us and we should be hanged. If it weren't for my husband's job, we wouldn't be here."[47]

—A gay father from South Carolina

Due to recent deadly attacks on LGBT clubs and social gatherings, many LGBT people have expressed concern and fear about gathering in places that they once felt safe, such as gay pride parades.

and we should be hanged. If it weren't for my husband's job, we wouldn't be here."[47]

After the Pulse nightclub shooting, many LGBT people and their families expressed fear about gathering in places that used to be safe or celebratory for the LGBT community, from gay bars to gay pride parades.

Ending the Violence

Since the recent dramatic increase in violence, many LGBT rights organizations have redoubled their efforts. These groups seek to document anti-LGBT violence, promote appropriate response and intervention, lead community safety and awareness campaigns, and ultimately end anti-LGBT violence. For example, the

New York's LGBT Monuments

In June 2016 the site of the historic Stonewall riots in New York City's Greenwich Village neighborhood was designated as the first US national monument dedicated to LGBT rights and history, managed by the National Park Service. That same month, in response to the Pulse nightclub attack, New York governor Andrew M. Cuomo formed the LGBT Memorial Commission to plan for the first official state monument to LGBT people, to be erected in New York City's Hudson River Park. The location, near the waterfront piers, has been a historic LGBT gathering place. The commission selected artist Anthony Goicolea to design the monument. Goicolea's design will present nine boulders, some of which use a glass prism to project rainbow patterns. These LGBT monuments honor the struggle for LGBT equal rights and commemorate victims and survivors of hate violence.

NCAVP provides community guides and tool kits to create support networks for rapid and appropriate response to violent incidents. These resources are especially needed in places where police protection is lacking. Communities Against Hate, overseen by a diverse coalition of organizations, is a national program that documents the often unreported stories of survivors and witnesses of hate crimes and connects them to legal resources and social services.

Several LGBT groups are specifically fighting the problem of transgender homicide. The National Center for Transgender Equality and FORGE, a national transgender antiviolence organization, provide resources to promote safer environments for transgender people, including a community resource manual for responding to hate crimes. Lambda Legal offers a transgender rights tool kit and legal guide for transgender people and their advocates. Communities across the world participate each year in the International Transgender Day of Remembrance on November 20 to raise public awareness of hate crimes and to honor victims. Unerased, a public database created by the NCAVP in collaboration with Mic, a media organization, also raises awareness about the prevalence of transgender murders.

In 2017, responding to the rise of hate-motivated violence and the reversal of LGBT state and federal legal protections, the NCAVP published *Platform to End Violence Against LGBT Communities*. The report states, "After 20 years of documenting violence against LGBTQ communities, we understand that all people, institutions, and movements working to end violence must not solely respond to violence, but also work to prevent it."[48] The report concludes by noting the urgency of ending violence against LGBTQ people, for the benefit and well-being of all people in society.

> "After 20 years of documenting violence against LGBTQ communities, we understand that all people, institutions, and movements working to end violence must not solely respond to violence, but also work to prevent it."[48]
>
> —The NCAVP

SOURCE NOTES

Introduction: LGBT in America: Both Personal and Public

1. Quoted in Emily Zak, "LGBPTTQQIIAA+—How We Got Here from Gay," *Ms. Magazine Blog*, *Ms.*, October 1, 2013. http://msmagazine.com.

Chapter 1: Is LGBT Discrimination Against the Law?

2. National LGBTQ Task Force, "The Pathway to Victory: A Review of Supreme Court LGBT Cases," 2018. www.thetaskforce.org.

3. Richard Socarides, "The Legacy of Edith Windsor," *New Yorker*, September 13, 2017. www.newyorker.com.

4. Debbie Cenziper and Jim Obergefell, *Love Wins: The Lovers and Lawyers Who Fought the Landmark Case for Marriage Equality*. New York: HarperCollins, 2015, p. 2.

5. Quoted in Michael S. Rosenwald, "How Jim Obergefell Became the Face of the Supreme Court Gay Marriage Case," *Washington Post*, April 6, 2015. www.washingtonpost.com.

6. Obergefell v. Hodges, 576 U.S. ___ (2015). https://supreme.justia.com.

7. Quoted in Robert D. McFadden, "Edith Windsor, Whose Same-Sex Marriage Fight Led to Landmark Ruling, Dies at 88," *New York Times*, September 12, 2017. www.nytimes.com.

8. Quoted in McFadden, "Edith Windsor, Whose Same-Sex Marriage Fight Led to Landmark Ruling, Dies at 88."

9. National Coalition of Anti-Violence Programs, *Lesbian, Gay, Bisexual, Transgender, Queer, and HIV-Affected Hate Violence in 2016*. New York: New York City Gay and Lesbian Anti-Violence Project, 2017. http://avp.org.

10. Frank Bruni, "The Worst (and Best) Places to Be Gay in America," *New York Times*, August 25, 2017. www.nytimes.com.

11. Human Rights Campaign, "Why the Equality Act?," 2018. www.hrc.org.

Chapter 2: LGBT Rights in Public Places

12. Quoted in Mary Emily O'Hara, "Gay Man Sues Funeral Home That Refused His 86-Year-Old Husband's Body," NBC News, May 3, 2017. www.nbcnews.com.
13. Quoted in Tanya Ballard Brown, "Did You Know It's Legal in Most States to Discriminate Against LGBT People?," *It's All Politics* (blog), NPR, April 28, 2015. www.npr.org.
14. Emma Green, "Can States Protect LGBT Rights Without Compromising Religious Freedom?," *Atlantic*, January 6, 2016. www.theatlantic.com.
15. Kim Davis, *Under God's Authority: The Kim Davis Story*. Maitland, FL: Liberty Counsel, 2018.
16. Alliance Defending Freedom, "You Are Free to Believe, but Are You Free to Act?," 2018. www.adflegal.org.
17. Quoted in US Commission on Civil Rights, *Peaceful Coexistence: Reconciling Nondiscrimination Principles with Civil Liberties*. Washington DC: US Commission on Civil Rights, 2016, p. 29. www.usccr.gov.
18. Quoted in Matt Ford, "Religious Liberty or Discrimination?," *Atlantic*, October 6, 2017. www.theatlantic.com.
19. Quoted in David G. Savage, "Colorado Cake Maker Asks Supreme Court to Provide a Religious Liberty Right to Refuse Gay Couple," *Los Angeles Times*, September 12, 2017. www.latimes.com.
20. Quoted in Alliance Defending Freedom, "Statement of Cake Artist Jack Phillips Following Oral Arguments at US Supreme Court," December 5, 2017. www.adfmedia.org.
21. Quoted in Nick Duffy, "Trump Administration Heads to Supreme Court to Support 'Freedom' to Discriminate Against Gay Customers," *PinkNews*, October 27, 2017. www.pink news.co.uk.
22. Quoted in Amber Phillips, "How Loretta Lynch's Speech Brought Some Transgender Advocates to Tears," *Washington Post*, May 11, 2016. www.washingtonpost.com.
23. Quoted in American Civil Liberties Union, "This Court Decision in the Gavin Grimm Case Will Bring Tears to Your Eyes," April 10, 2017. www.aclu.org.

24. GLAAD, "The 2016 Election: Know the Facts About the Equality Act." www.glaad.org.

Chapter 3: Special Issues for LGBT Youth

25. Quoted in Jen Doll, "A New Way for Gay Characters in Y.A.," *Atlantic*, March 28, 2013. www.theatlantic.com.
26. Mark Meinke, "Why LGBT Historic Sites Matter," in *LGBTQ America: A Theme Study of Lesbian, Gay, Bisexual, Transgender, and Queer History*, ed. Megan E. Springate. Washington, DC: National Park Foundation, 2016. www.nps.gov.
27. Quoted in Shannon Keating, "Coming Out as Gay in Elementary School," BuzzFeed, April 27, 2015. www.buzzfeed.com.
28. Quoted in Human Rights Campaign, *Growing Up LGBT in America*. Washington, DC: Human Rights Campaign, 2012. www.hrc.org.
29. Quoted in Human Rights Watch, "Like Walking Through a Hailstorm," December 7, 2016. www.hrw.org.
30. Quoted in Human Rights Campaign, *Growing Up LGBT in America*.
31. Jordan Dashow, "On #40toNoneDay, HRC Youth Ambassador Shares His Experience with Homelessness," Human Rights Campaign, April 26, 2017. www.hrc.org.
32. Quoted in Marissa Higgins, "LGBT Students Are Not Safe at School," *Atlantic*, October 18, 2016. www.theatlantic.com.
33. Quoted in Human Rights Watch, "Like Walking Through a Hailstorm."

Chapter 4: Discrimination in Employment and the Workplace

34. Quoted in Sejal Singh and Laure E. Durso, "Widespread Discrimination Continues to Shape LGBT People's Lives in Both Subtle and Significant Ways," Center for American Progress, May 2, 2017. www.americanprogress.org.
35. Quoted in Singh and Durso, "Widespread Discrimination Continues to Shape LGBT People's Lives in Both Subtle and Significant Ways."
36. Quoted in Darran Simon, "Lesbian Plaintiff in Work Discrimination Suit Sticking to Fight," CNN, April 5, 2017. www.cnn.com.

37. Quoted in Simon, "Lesbian Plaintiff in Work Discrimination Suit Sticking to Fight."
38. Quoted in Vanessa Chestnut, "Plaintiff at Center of Landmark Gay-Rights Case Never Got to Witness His Victory," NBC News, March 3, 2018. www.nbcnews.com.
39. Quoted in Robert Pear, "Transgender Workers Gain New Protection Under Court Ruling," *New York Times*, March 24, 2018. www.nytimes.com.
40. Tim Cook, "Tim Cook Speaks Up," *Bloomberg Businessweek*, October 30, 2014. www.bloomberg.com.
41. Quoted in Garrett Epps, "Trump's Tweets Take Down His Military Ban on Trans People," *Atlantic*, November 1, 2017. www.theatlantic.com.
42. Quoted in US Commission on Civil Rights, *Working for Inclusion: Time for Congress to Enact Federal Legislation to Address Workplace Discrimination Against Lesbian, Gay, Bisexual, and Transgender Americans*. Washington, DC: US Commission on Civil Rights, 2017. www.usccr.gov.

Chapter 5: Violence Against LGBT People

43. Quoted in Associated Press, "Orlando Massacre: Son's Heartbreaking Texts Reveal Final Moments," NBC News, June 13, 2016. www.nbcnews.com.
44. Quoted in Haeyoun Park and Iaryna Mykhyalyshyn, "L.G.B.T. People Are More Likely to Be Targets of Hate Crimes than Any Other Minority Group," *New York Times*, June 16, 2016. www.nytimes.com.
45. National Coalition of Anti-Violence Programs, *Lesbian, Gay, Bisexual, Transgender, Queer, and HIV-Affected Hate Violence in 2016*. New York: NCAVP, 2017. http://avp.org.
46. US Department of Justice, "Hate Crimes." www.justice.gov.
47. Quoted in Bruni, "The Worst (and Best) Places to Be Gay in America."
48. National Coalition of Anti-Violence Programs, *Platform to End Violence Against LGBTQ Communities*. New York: New York City Gay and Lesbian Anti-Violence Project, 2017. http://avp .org.

ORGANIZATIONS AND WEBSITES

Alliance Defending Freedom
15100 N. Ninetieth St.
Scottsdale, AZ 85260
website: www.adflegal.org

Alliance Defending Freedom is a highly influential Christian organization that funds cases, trains lawyers, and advocates for religious freedom, sanctity of life, marriage, and family. Its position against LGBT rights is explained on its website, along with the campaign to support Masterpiece Cakeshop in the religious liberty Supreme Court case.

Family Research Council (FRC)
801 G St. NW
Washington, DC 20001
website: www.frc.org

The FRC is a prominent conservative Christian organization that seeks to advance traditional family values through lobbying and advocacy. The FRC publicly opposes LGBT rights legislation and supports religious liberty. Position papers and analyses are found in the "Homosexuality" and "Religious Liberty" website areas.

Federal Bureau of Investigation (FBI)
FBI Headquarters
935 Pennsylvania Ave. NW
Washington, DC 20535
website: www.fbi.gov

The FBI investigates and seeks to prevent hate crimes, including crimes based on bias regarding sexual orientation and gender identity. Detailed annual statistics for US hate crimes are published annually in reports on the FBI website.

GLSEN

110 William St., 30th Floor
New York, NY 10038
website: www.glsen.org

GLSEN is a national organization that works to make K–12 schools safe for LGBT students. The organization oversees a US network of chapters, student clubs, and educators. The GLSEN website includes research reports, relevant laws and policies, lesson plans and professional development tools, student programs, model antibullying policies, and more.

Human Rights Campaign

1640 Rhode Island Ave. NW
Washington, DC 20036
website: www.hrc.org

The Human Rights Campaign is the largest US civil rights organization advocating for the rights of LGBTQ Americans. It tracks national developments that impact LGBTQ rights, lists upcoming advocacy events, and provides information and reports on LGBT topics, community resources and tool kits, and a list of the organization's youth ambassadors.

Movement Advancement Project

3020 Carbon Place, Suite 202
Boulder, CO 80301
website: www.lgbtmap.org

The Movement Advancement Project is an independent think tank that produces and publishes on its website research and analysis related to LGBT issues. The website also features interactive "Equality Maps" that map the geographical distribution of LGBT policies, laws, and issues in the country as a whole and in specific states.

National Center for Transgender Equality

1133 Nineteenth St. NW, Suite 302
Washington, DC 20036
website: https://transequality.org

The National Center for Transgender Equality advocates for the rights of transgender people in the United States, focusing on policy change advocacy and media activism. The website contains research reports, advocacy opportunities, information about understanding transgender people, and discussions of relevant social issues and civil rights.

National Coalition of Anti-Violence Programs (NCAVP)

116 Nassau St., 3rd Floor
New York, NY 10038
website: https://avp.org/ncavp

The NCAVP oversees local programs that seek to prevent, respond to, and ultimately end violence against LGBT people. The NCAVP publishes its two annual reports about anti-LGBT violence on its website, along with action briefs, tool kits, and information about a hotline and other forms of support.

Trevor Project

PO Box 69232
West Hollywood, CA 90069
website: www.thetrevorproject.org

The Trevor Project provides suicide prevention services for LGBTQ individuals aged thirteen to thirty-four. The website provides information about crisis intervention with live professional counselors (by phone, chat, and text), prevention training and resource materials, and community resources such as online training modules and model school policies.

Williams Institute

UCLA School of Law
Box 951476
Los Angeles, CA 90095
website: https://williamsinstitute.law.ucla.edu

The Williams Institute is a think tank at the University of California–Los Angeles School of Law that conducts and publishes independent research on LGBT issues and demographics that relate to laws and public policy. Research reports on a wide range of topics are available on its website.

FOR FURTHER RESEARCH

Books

Debbie Cenziper and Jim Obergefell, *Love Wins: The Lovers and Lawyers Who Fought the Landmark Case for Marriage Equality*. New York: Morrow, 2016.

Alex Cooper with Joanna Brooks, *Saving Alex: When I Was Fifteen I Told My Parents I Was Gay and That's When My Nightmare Began*. New York: HarperOne, 2016.

Lillian Faderman, *The Gay Revolution: The Story of the Struggle*. New York: Simon & Schuster, 2015.

Brittney Griner, *In My Skin: My Life On and Off the Basketball Court*. New York: It, 2016.

Damon Karson, *Human Rights in Focus: The LGBT Community*. San Diego: ReferencePoint, 2018.

Betsy Maury, ed., *The Reference Shelf: LGBTQ in the 21st Century*. Ipswich, MA: Wilson, 2017.

Pat Rarus, *The LGBT Rights Movement*. San Diego: ReferencePoint, 2019.

Robert Rodi and Laura Ross, *Being Transgender*. Broomall, PA: Mason Crest, 2017.

Susan Stryker, *Transgender History: The Roots of Today's Revolution*. 2nd ed. New York: Seal, 2017.

Internet Sources

Emma Green, "Can States Protect LGBT Rights Without Compromising Religious Freedom?," *Atlantic*, January 6, 2016. www.theatlantic.com/politics/archive/2016/01/lgbt-discrimination-protection-states-religion/422730.

Human Rights Watch, "Like Walking Through a Hailstorm," December 7, 2016. www.hrw.org/report/2016/12/07/walking-through-hailstorm/discrimination-against-lgbt-youth-us-schools.

Movement Advancement Project, *LGBT Policy Spotlight: Public Accommodations Nondiscrimination Laws*. Boulder, CO: Movement Advancement Project, 2018. www.lgbtmap.org/file/Spotlight-Public-Accommodations-FINAL.pdf.

National Coalition of Anti-Violence Programs, *Lesbian, Gay, Bisexual, Transgender, Queer, and HIV-Affected Hate Violence in 2016*. New York: New York City Gay and Lesbian Anti-Violence Project, 2017. http://avp.org/wp-content/uploads/2017/06/NCAVP_2016HateViolence_REPORT.pdf.

Sejal Singh and Laure E. Durso, "Widespread Discrimination Continues to Shape LGBT People's Lives in Both Subtle and Significant Ways," Center for American Progress, May 2, 2017. www.americanprogress.org/issues/lgbt/news/2017/05/02/429529/widespread-discrimination-continues-shape-lgbt-peoples-lives-subtle-significant-ways.

Megan E. Springate, ed., *LGBTQ America: A Theme Study of Lesbian, Gay, Bisexual, Transgender, and Queer History*. Washington, DC: National Park Foundation, 2016. www.nps.gov/subjects/lgbtqheritage/upload/lgbtqtheme-prologue.pdf.

US Commission on Civil Rights, *Working for Inclusion: Time for Congress to Enact Federal Legislation to Address Workplace Discrimination Against Lesbian, Gay, Bisexual, and Transgender Americans*. Washington, DC: US Commission on Civil Rights, 2017. www.usccr.gov/pubs/LGBT_Employment_Discrimination2017.pdf.

INDEX